DREAM INTERPRETER

Presented to

Samuel

From

Dr. Bailey L. Bartlett

Date

_11-16-19_

DREAM INTERPRETER

Barbie L. Breathitt, Ph.D.

Books by Dr. Barbie L. Breathitt

Dream Encounters: Seeing Your Destiny from God's Perspective

Gateway to the Seer Realm: Look Again to See Beyond the Natural

So You Want to Change the World?

Hearing and Understanding the Voice of God

Dream Seer: Searching for the Face of the Invisible

Dream Interpreter

A to Z Dream Symbology Dictionary

Volume I Dream Symbols

Volume II Dream Symbols

Volume III Dream Symbols

Action Dream Symbols

When Will My Dreams Come True?
Dream Interpretation Nuggets, Times & Seasons

Dream Sexology

Sports & Recreation Dream Symbols

DREAM INTERPRETER

© Copyright 2014–Barbie Breathitt Enterprises All rights reserved.

This book is protected by the copyright laws of the United States of America. This book may not be copied or reprinted for commercial gain or profit. The use of short quotations or occasional page copying for personal or group study is permitted and encouraged. Permission will be granted upon request. Unless otherwise identified, Scripture quotations are taken from the NEW AMERICAN STANDARD BIBLE®, Copyright©1960, 1962, 1963,1968,1971,1972,1973, 1975,1977,1995 by The Lockman Foundation. Used by permission. Scripture quotations marked NKJV are taken from the New King James Version. Copyright © 1982 by Thomas Nelson, Inc. Used by permission. All rights reserved. Scripture quotations marked NIV are taken from the HOLY BIBLE, NEW INTER NATIONAL VERSION®, Copyright © 1973, 1978, 1984 International Bible Society. Used by permission of Zondervan. All rights reserved. Scripture quotations marked MSG are taken from The Message. Copyright © 1993, 1994, 1995, 1996, 2000, 2001, 2002. Used by permission of NavPress Publishing Group. Scripture quotations marked AMP are taken from the Amplified® Bible, Copyright © 1954, 1958, 1962, 1964, 1965, 1987 by The Lockman Foundation. Used by permission. Scripture quotations marked NLT are taken from the Holy Bible, New Living Translation, copyright 1996, 2004. Used by permission of Tyndale House Publishers., Wheaton, Illinois 60189. All rights reserved. Scripture quotations marked KJV are taken from the King James Version. Scripture quotations marked CJB are taken from the Complete Jewish Bible, copyright © 1998 by David H. Stern. Published by Jewish New Testament Publications, Inc. www.messianicjewish.net/jntp. Distributed by Messianic Jewish Resources Int'l. www.messianicjewish.net. All rights reserved. Used by permission. Scripture quotations marked ERV are taken from the Easy to- Read Version Copyright ©2006 World Bible Translation Center. Used by permission. All rights reserved.

All rights reserved. No part of this publication may be reproduced, stored in a retrieval system, or transmitted in any form or by any means, electronic, mechanical, photocopying, recording, or otherwise, without the prior written permission of the publisher.

Breath of the Spirit Ministries, Inc.
P.O. Box 820653
North Richland Hills, Texas 76182–0653
www.BarbieBreathitt.com
www.BarbieBreathittEnterprises.com
www.MyOnar.com

ISBN-13: 978-1-60-383257-2

ISBN 1603832572

Published by: Barbie Breathitt Enterprises, Inc.

Printed in Canada

Dedication

DREAM INTERPRETER is dedicated to my dearly beloved life-long best friend and confidant Joy Biggers. She has been instrumental in my spiritual growth and development, as iron has sharpened iron. We have ministered and traveled together on many occasions. Dr. Joy Biggers is licensed and ordained with Breath of the Spirit Ministries, Inc. as our Senior Instructor. She teaches all of our Encounter courses: including but not limited to Dream Encounters, Healing Encounters, Revelatory Encounter, Kingdom Encounter and the Angelic Encounters series. She is very gifted in the prophetic, having served on and led ministry teams for over 35 years. She has been the Senior Dream Interpreter and Administrator for www.MyOnar.com, Breath of the Spirit's exceptional dream interpretation and training site for over twelve years. Joy's intellect and quick wit makes her a very popular conference speaker. She will have the audience laughing and crying as the Spirit of God moves in deep revelation. Joy was born on November 1, 1944 in Dayton, Ohio and graduated Bellbrook High School in 1962. Joy holds several academic degrees, a Bachelor of Arts in English from College of Mt. Saint Joseph in Cincinnati, Ohio in 1964. She attended Ohio State University in Columbus, Ohio. She then went onto Loyola University, Chicago, Illinois to earn a Masters of Education, and Bachelor of Arts graduating in 1974. Joy's love for learning led her to Florida Atlantic University in Boca Raton, where she graduated as a Specialist in Administration and Supervision in 1989. She continued her education at Life Christian University in Lutz, Fla. graduating in 2012 where she is currently on staff as a professor. Dr. Biggers retired after serving from 1975 until 2008 as the principal of two public elementary schools in Polk County, Fla. She is the mother of two children Angel and Thomas Zigman. She is also the proud grandmother of two beautiful grand daughters. Joy lives in Lakeland, Fla. with her husband Randy Biggers. They instruct the youthful offenders and inmates in the maximum security Sumter Correctional Institution in Bushnell, Fla. while also training teams to minister in Bartow, Florida's women's jails.

DREAM INTERPRETER

Endorsements

Most of us who are true believers want to hear the voice of God when He has something to say to us. However, Barbie Breathitt, through her fascinating book Dream Interpreter, has alerted me to the fact that I might be missing some of what God has been saying because I have not been properly tuned into the wave lengths of my dreams. This persuasive book takes people like me into new realms of reality, namely how God uses our dream life to hear His voice more clearly, to be activated into new levels of service, and to fulfill His destiny for us. After you read Dream Seer you will never be the same!

C. Peter Wagner, Vice-President Global Spheres, Inc.

I want to highly recommend to you this amazing new book by Barbie Breathitt called the Dream Interpreter. In her book Barbie shares incredible revelation and insight into the understanding and function of the world of dreams. As a leading voice in the Body of Christ in Dreams and interpretation, and understanding dream language, Barbie brings a fresh revelation that is easy to understand and digest. I want to highly recommend this book for all church leaders and those with supernatural schools who are hungry for more and are looking to teach and bring understanding into the realm of seeing into the Supernatural Kingdom of God. This is a must read!

Jeff Jansen
Global Fire Ministries International
Senior Leader Global Fire Church
Global Connect Churches
Kingdom Life Institute

Barbie Breathitt of Breath of the Spirit Ministries has done it again! Few people I know can merge together such bodies of truth and convey it in such a manner that the everyday person can comprehend. In the book Dream Interpreter, Barbie takes you on a journey that is deep and wide at the same time. By combining understanding from scripture, physiological truths, the science of the brain all with a prophetic edge that penetrates any resistance. Well done! Amazing!

James Goll
Encounters Network • Prayer Storm • God Encounters Training
Best Selling Author of The Seer, The Lost Art of Intercession,
Dream Language and many more.

Barbie Breathitt does an excellent job of linking the move of God in our lives with the dreams that He places in us. Barbie uncovers for us God's divine revelation of who each of us have been destined to be! Your life-dreams will be unraveled and made clear, for she writes as a prophetic sage, full of wisdom gained through years of experience. Dream Interpreter will show you that your life has been created to experience God, and Barbie will show you how! Sprinkled with true life stories that will capture your attention she brings before you the power of spiritual transformation from a godly perspective. Curious about your destiny and the path God has placed you on? Then DREAM INTERPRETER is for you! Read it and enjoy the journey!

Dr. Brian Simmons
Stairway Ministries & The Passion Translation Project

I believe Barbie Breathitt's new book, Dream Interpreter, will stir you to pursue the things of the spirit with a hunger to hear the voice of God through Dreams and Visions. She writes that Dreams have the power to awaken us to our destiny. This book is a revelatory key that will certainly empower you to be led by the Spirit and to help fulfill the will of God in your life.

Adam F Thompson
Co-Author of "The Divinity Code to Understanding Your Dreams & Visions"
www.thedivinitycode.org,
Co-Planter of "Field of Dreams Australia"
www.fieldofdreams.org.au

Barbie's book, Dream Interpreter, is a topically-packed handbook filled with insights that empower the reader to better understand and participate with God in seeing their dreams become reality. In this book she also imparts wisdom and revelation beyond mere dream interpretation to see champions raised for the kingdom. A must read for all hungry to see heaven on earth.

Adrian Beale
Co-Author of "The Divinity Code to Understanding Your Dreams & Visions"
thedivinitycode.org
everrestministries.com

Dream Interpreter is an in-depth study tool, skillfully including the subjects of dreams and the seer anointing from a biblical perspective. It is EXCELLENT! This book is a must for your library. Those who sit under Barbie Breathitt's empowering prophetic teaching ministry gain a great increase in their understanding of how God speaks through revelations, dreams, and visions. The seer anointing is bound to awaken in your life as you read Dream Interpreter.

Patricia King
Founder, XPministries

Within the pages of this book Dr. Barbie Breathitt effectively takes us on a journey of unlocking prophetic gifts of God within us. She has the ability to impart to us the depth of wisdom and divine understanding she has gleaned over the years of proven prophetic ministry. You will be supernaturally stirred, gain deeper insight, be filled with Spirit-breathed vision and have many "ah ha" moments as you read. "I highly recommend this revelatory resource. It should be a part of every spiritual seeker library– I've already made it part of mine!"

Joshua Mills
Best Selling Author of "31 Days to a Miracle Mindset" Palm Springs, Canada, California and London www.JoshuaMills.com

Barbie's life's work in the ministry thus far can be summarized in two words: inhaling & exhaling... Inhaling a vast amount of scripture and study and exhaling a prolific volume of teachings and blessings. The multitudes that have been touched by her ministry are impressive and the testimonies are real. My hope and prayer is that her book Dream Interpreter will touch YOU.

Karl Zimmerman
Senior Wealth Advisor
Director of Wealth Management
Oakville, Ontario

Table of Contents

Books by Dr. Barbie L. Breathitt i
Dedication iii
Endorsements v
Foreword xiii
Introduction xvii
Chapter 1 Dreams 1
    Dreams are Symbolic Night Parables 2
    Dreams Tell You Who You Are 3
    Dreams are Mirror Images of the Soul 3
    Dreams Reveal Unforgiveness and Negative Feelings 3
    Revelation Knowledge 4
    Four Sleep Cycles 5
    Times and Seasons 6
Chapter 2 Visions of the Night 21
    Dream Seer 21
    Dream Symbolism 23
    Interpreting Dreams 24
    Prophetic or Precognitive Dreams 28
    Common Ordinary Dreams 30
    Occult or False Dreams 31
Chapter 3 Nightmares 33
    Description of Nightmares 34
    Why Nightmares? 34
    What Causes Nightmares? 35
    Benefits of Nightmares 37

    From Darkness I Was Taken 38
    Frequent Nightmares 40
    Listen to Your Nightmares 40
    REM Nightmares 42
    Physical Paralysis 42
    Facing Your Fears 43
    Freedom from Nightmares 44
    Panic Attacks 45
    Nightmares in Children 47

Chapter 4 Night Terrors 49
    Night Terrors in Children 49
    Symptoms of Night Terrors 50
    Delivered from Night Terrors 53
    REM Sleep Behavior Disorders 55
    Characteristics of RBD 55
    Confusional Arousal Disorder 56

Chapter 5 Sleepwalking 57
    Causes of Sleepwalking 57
    Treatments of Sleepwalking 58
    Counting Sheep.....Will I Ever Sleep? 59
    Wet Dreams 60

Chapter 6 Animals & Creatures Great and Small 63
    Monster Mania 64

Chapter 7 Body Dreams 65
    Fee 66
    Growths or Wounds 68
    Losing Limbs 69
    Legs 69
    Broken Hearted or Breakthrough? 70
    Heart Issues 71
    Don't Lose Your Head! 72
    Brain Pain 72
    Hair Brain 73
    Devoured by a Wild Beast 74
    Receiving New Body Parts 74
    Helping or Hurtful Hands 76
    The Face 77
    The Liver 78
    The Mouth 78
    The Nose Knows 78
    Muscles 79
    Paralysis 79
    Pregnancy 79

Shoulder	80
The Skin	80
The Spine	80
The Throat	81

Chapter 7 Buildings, Rooms & Structures 83

The Attic	85
The Basement	85
The Backyard	86
The Bathroom	86
Flush the Toilet	87
Where's the Toilet?	87
Showering or Bathing	88
Coiffuring	88
Razor Sharp	88
It's Time to Make-up not Cover-up	89
The Bedroom	89
Buildings	89
Foundational Issues	90
Corridor	90
Doors	90
Front Yard or Porch	92
The Home	92
The Kitchen	92
The Living Room	93
The Hallway	93
Passageway	94
Past Homes or Dwellings	94
Windows	95

Chapter 8 Frequent Dream Categories 97

Anger	97
Murder	98
Drowning	98
Running Away or Chasing Dreams	98
Out of Control	99
I Can't Find My Purse or Wallet	99
Lost Identity	103
Lost Again	104
Tornadoes Disaster Strikes	107
The Storms of Life	109
Dreams Reveal our Internal Questions,	110
Talents & Treasures	110
Warfare Dreams	111
Funeral Dreams	112
Death, Trauma or Bereavement Dreams	113

    Shame and Guilt Dreams 114
    Betrayal and Rejection 115
    Inner Vows 123
    Got the Job! 124
    Overcoming Rejection 126

Chapter 9 Common Dreams and Dream Symbols 129

Chapter 10 People are Significant 135
    What in the World Are You Wearing? 139
    So You Are Pregnant Again! 140
    What if You Really are Pregnant? 140

Chapter 11 Puns and Word Plays 143
    Puns 144
    Word Plays 145

Chapter 12 Food and Nutrition Dream Symbols 147
    Food is Essential 148
    Meat 150
    Vegetables 150
    Frozen Food 151
    Baby Food 152
    Milk 153
    Food Can Talk 155
    God's Amazing Food Pharmacy 155
    Pharaoh's Grain and Cattle Dreams 162

Author Bio 165

Foreword

In every circumstance we are in, we must find God's sovereignty in that circumstance and be faithful to walk in His will. One of the primary ways that God has always used to communicate with His people is through dreams and visions, yet they are often misunderstood, dismissed, or ignored. Dreams particularly can seem foolish or strange. In 1 Cor. 1:27, Paul said that God chose the foolish things of the world to confound the wise. Although many dreams are foolish or senseless to the world, they are precious to those who understand 'the hidden wisdom' from above.

The Old Testament is laden with dream scenes and interpretations. In the Bible we actually find over 50 references for messages being sent by God through dreams and visions, to both the righteous and the unrighteous alike. The Lord used dreams and visions to guide, to warn, to direct, to help – to communicate His heart. God has not stopped communicating to humanity by these means. In fact, God often uses dreams and visions to reach unsaved individuals with the Gospel, particularly in closed parts of the world. We have scores of testimonies of dreams and visions being used by God to draw individuals, families, and entire communities to Himself. Similarly, the Lord uses this method of revelation in the lives of most, if not all, believers.

What is a Dream?

A dream is a release of revelation (whether natural or spiritual) that comes at a time when your body is at peace and you are settled. Sometimes this is the only way God can communicate with us, because our soul is quiet enough for the Lord to speak deeply into our spirit man. A dream is like a photograph of something you are able to relate to in a movie form. Ecclesiastes 5:3 tells us that a dream comes when there are many cares.

Dreams are formed in a person's subconscious mind. They are based on the imagery and secret symbolic language that are exclusive and strategic to that person's particular life and destiny. Dreams can either be a subconscious response to the circumstances of our lives or the Holy Spirit communicating His plans, ways and purposes to us. Dreams enable us to tap into the superior ways of the Divine Spirit. Dreams enable us to glance into the imperceptible realms of wisdom, counsel, knowledge and might.

The dreams and visions God births in us bring revelation, illumination, and inspiration. When we accept delivery of God's dream letters of love, He releases the strategic power to change every life event into something wonderful. He turns negative happenings to our advantage and improvement. Dreams enable us to glance into the imperceptible realms of wisdom, counsel, knowledge and might.

Dreams Can Reveal the Future

In the ancient eastern world, dreams were treated as reality. Dreams were the world of the divine or the demonic. They often revealed the future. Dreams could be filled with revelation that would cause the dreamer to make the right decision for his/her future. For instance, I once had a dream because I was in prayer over a trip to Israel. Barbara Byerly and I were going to be leading prayer for a meeting that would reconcile Arab Christian leaders and Messianic leaders. Dr. Peter Wagner was going to be facilitating this meeting. There was much warfare surrounding this meeting. I became very anxious and called Barbara and told her we should pray and fast for three days before going. Barbara was having the same burden and agreed immediately.

In the second day of the fast I fell asleep and had the following dream: Barbara Wentroble, a well-known prophetess, was in the dream and asked me a question. "So, you are going to Israel. There are two ways. Which way are you taking?" I told her the way we were going. In the dream it was as if I was showing her a map and we were wandering through the Arab desert to get to Israel. She then said, "You may go that way, but if you do, you will experience much warfare. There is a better way for you to take." I said, "Oh, what is that way?" She replied, "Go straight to Israel and meet with the leadership you know. Then, have your meeting with everyone else." I woke up and knew I had revelation that God had spoken to me to give me direction for Dr. Wagner as he proceeded in pulling together this meeting. I encouraged him to first have a meeting with the leaders of Israel that we knew. Then we could have the overall meeting and reconciliation time. This proved to be straight revelation from God and really affected the overall outcome of our mission.

Israel was forbidden to use many of the same type of divining practices as Egypt and other neighboring countries and peoples. However, God would visit them in the night to communicate His will and way to them. This continued through the changing of covenants, from old to new. In the first two chapters of the New Testament, God gives direction through prophetic dreams five times.

Always Talk to God About Your Dreams

Exercising discernment is very important in determining the source of dreams and visions. Without this, we can be basing our life decisions on soulish desires, or the enemy could gain a ready inroad to thwart us in our destiny. No matter what the origin of a dream we have had, we can and should always talk to the Lord about what we have dreamed. Prophets such as Jeremiah and Zechariah cautioned about dreams not being filled with God's word (see Jer. 23:25–27; Zech.10:2). Jeremiah placed dreamers with soothsayers, sorcerers and false prophets (see Jer. 27:9). Therefore, he equated some dreams to false prophecy. God was warning through the prophets that people could begin to rely on dreams and not seek God's word for truth. So, not only could God reveal His will through dreams, but there was a warning not to just rely on this method to know the will of God.

We should not ignore what a dream may reveal about our emotions, and can always ask God to clarify puzzling or disturbing dreams so He can bring His comfort and healing to our mind, will, and emotions. If we discern that a dream is demonic in nature, it might be an indication of how the enemy is working to thwart us, or could be a call to a new level of spiritual warfare. All dreams have some level of significance in our lives, and it is important to invite the Lord into the process of determining what the level of significance of each dream may be. That is why the book you are holding in your hands is so valuable!

Dr. Barbie Breathitt is one of the best teachers there is on dream interpretation, and for decoding the symbols and code the Lord can use when communicating with His people. Her latest book, Dream Interpreter, will encourage you to believe your destiny is designed in the language of your dreams, visions and imagination, so anything is possible when God is present. God fashioned His glorious image, splendid character and grand imagination within each Believer so that our identity and nature is caught up in Christ. When our hearts feel God's emotions and our minds mirror His thoughts, we live and move in His presence to become a reflection of His greatness on earth.

As Barbie shares, dreams enable us to see the plans and purposes God had for us before we entered into this earthly realm of existence. All of our days were numbered and ordered before we were born. Part of our spiritual journey is learning how to enter into the divine scripts of success that have already been written for each of us in our dreams. Dreams bring the revelation of who we are to become in Christ once our spirit is awakened, our soul is born again, and then enlightened by the Holy Spirit. This revelation enables each believer to work together as a unit, while keeping our individuality. We each have a component and diverse function that is displayed through the corporate body of Christ, in the progression of life.

Dreams awaken our mind's vision to the unlimited possibilities that await us. Nothing is impossible when we attach ourselves to the power of God's love. We are created in God's image. Therefore, we possess the same power to create with our visual images and words. The dreams we envision grant us agreement with Heaven to remove any obstacle that would constrain us to be common. Dream Interpreter will cause a dimension of your seeing through night visions and dreams to come alive. As you read this book, expect to find yourself walking and living in a faith realm BEYOND where you have ever been before!

Dr. Chuck D. Pierce
President, Global Spheres Inc.
President, Glory of Zion Intl.

Introduction

There is only one right interpretation, God's; every thing else is only shades of gray. When we seek and find God's presence our perception is opened to know His present will for us. However if we do not search for God's interpretation of life's events we are captured by complacency the enemy of spiritual hunger that robs us of all desire. Without a desperate desire to know God, and an accurate interpretation of God there will be no manifestation of God. When God appears we learn to love because God first loved us. When we love God passionately with our whole heart, barriers are removed and the distance of eternity fades away.

An interpreter is one who gives an explanation, account or translates an event or happening in either written or oral expressions translating it from one language into another. An interpreter is able to decode symbols, types and shadows of images in order to render, crack or explain the hidden mysteries that are contained within. The gifted interpreter can decipher, convert and transform a concealed secret and turn it into a blue print for prosperity to be shared by the hearer.

Job 33:23–26 speaks of an interpreter in this manner, "If there be an angelic messenger who is watching over him, or an interpreter of dreams, visions and mysteries, they are so rare only one among a thousand, to show unto man his uprightness: Then he is gracious unto him, and saith, Deliver him from going down to the pit: I have found a ransom. His flesh shall be fresher than a child's: he shall return to the days of his youth: he shall pray unto God, and he will be favorable unto him: and he shall see his face with joy, for he will render unto man his righteousness."

DREAM INTERPRETER

Chapter 1
Dreams

Dreams come to visit every night as a wise counselor or friend. They present the truth about one's life in a vivid or graphic way through a picture language. Each night a dream evolves and is fashioned from the depths of one's soul potential. These dreams reveal one's individual needs, wants, and desires. Dreams come to guide the dreamer through life.

The Holy Spirit, as a messenger, comes to visit and express Himself to the spirit of man during the solemn hours of the night. The soul of man diligently searches for the Spirit of God at night. God is the One who gave us being; so He is our eternal source of life, everything we have and everything we are comes from Him.

The soul knows the truth so it resonates with the spirit of truth that is in God. When truth is presented to the soul, truth will bring a fullness of understanding, the divine purpose for which the soul was born. Our soul wanders many paths at night looking for God's light and listening for His voice. When our soul finds God's illuminating light, it memorizes the paths that brought it to God. Once the path is discovered the soul can return night after night to gain truth, spiritual enlightenment, and godly understanding. Dreams and visions come to guide our soul to God, the giver of life and destiny. The soul is enlightened by the wisdom it receives from dreams. Godly wisdom enables people to follow a call to excellence and dignity.

The path of wisdom leads us to the God of all wisdom and knowledge. The light of God's knowledge is a shining beacon that inspires us to understand the mysteries that have been sealed in the heart of God and in the heart of each person from the beginning of time.

Dreams are Symbolic Night Parables

Jesus is the greatest storyteller. He has the ability to tap into the creative imagination of a crowd. Imagination and faith are at completely different poles of opinion. Imagination is not faith; it summons unreal images in the mind as they assemble a dreamlike story or an amazing parable forms. The words of Jesus' mouth painted a brilliant scene that enabled those, who had eyes to see, and ears to hear, to enter into a level of wisdom they had never experienced before. Jesus often taught people by using parables. He told stories that related to their culture and the everyday lives of individuals. Jesus sought to captivate their hearts. He related how His heavenly kingdom operated on a much higher level of faith in comparison to the traditions of the day.

Faith unlike imagination creates nothing, but reveals that which already exist in the invisible realm. The parables Jesus shared had many levels of knowledge and layered insights into the invisible realm of reality. The words of wisdom Jesus shared brought His listeners into a deeper spiritual and moral meaning of life. The blindness of the hardhearted is healed when the powerful light of truth, revealed by the Spirit, becomes real. Jesus' disciples asked, *"Why do You speak to them in parables?"* He admonished His disciples that they must be able to interpret parables and understand this type of symbolic thinking in order to uncover the mysteries and hidden treasures of the kingdom of heaven. *"Because it has been given unto you to know the mysteries of the kingdom of heaven, but to them [the world] it has not been given ... But blessed are your eyes for they see, and your ears for they hear; for surely, I say to you that many prophets and righteous men desired to see what you see, and did not see it, and to hear what you hear, and did not hear it (Matthew 13:10–17)."*

It is the same for us today. Jesus still teaches us through parables but now they come in a different form, they come through the dreams of the night. These mysteries are hidden in the realms of the Spirit. When we shift from focusing on the seen, to centering on the unseen God, He becomes the Spirit of Truth and manifests as a daily reality. It has been given to us to know the mysteries, but we must develop our spiritual eyes and ears to truly hear and see correctly. God is a Spirit. Therefore, as worshippers of God, we must diligently seek His presence to worship Him in Spirit and in truth to enter into the rewards of the realm of mystical understanding and enlightenment. It is the Spirit of truth that leads and guides us into the vast dimension of God's truth. The spiritual world of God, though invisible to our natural eyes, is the real truth. Our natural senses do not appeal to our faith; but, jealously demand our constant focused attention, drawing us away from the subtly of the Holy Spirit's whispers. The visible collides with the invisible; the temporal with the eternal, yet the Christian wisely believes and places their faith in the unseen magnificent God.

Dreams Tell You Who You Are

People who are serious about hearing from God about their life, destiny and personal giftings should submit their dreams to me on www.MyOnar.com for interpretation. Dreams not only tell you who you were in the past, who you are now, the gifts and callings you possess, but they also tell who you are destined to become. Similar to the powers of our imagination, dreaming is a universal human phenomenon uniting people across barriers of age, gender, racial background, social differences, religious beliefs and historical circumstances. Dreams are our inner man at work revealing our true nature to us. The Scriptures beckons us to rise into the realm of another world's light, to renew the mind and to quicken our mortal spirit. Believers should not wait until they die to learn how to move into success by understanding spiritual things. Now is the time to learn how to relate to the spiritual realms of God. What we learn here on earth will insure we are that much further along in our training process once we enter into heaven.

Dreams are Mirror Images of the Soul

Dreams are a mirror image of the soul and reflect our inner condition by revealing what will transpire if positive changes do or do not take place in us. The kind of attitude we have and the emphasis and value we place on dreams will determine the beneficial results we will receive from them. Dreams are like relationships we maintain with friends. If we nurture them and pay attention to them, they will grow, blossom and develop. If we ignore and neglect them they will dry up, vaporize and disappear. If we listen to them, write them down and have them interpreted, keeping their insights in an online journal, and then follow their instruction, dreams become a counselor to us. But if we ignore our dreams and never search out the meanings of our dreams, we will not flourish. Dreams are a visual depiction of the untapped potential that lies within the human soul.

The symbols that appear in our dreams are spiritual indicators of our current level of godly intimacy and relationship, as well our natural state of affairs. Dreams reveal areas in our life where we are and are not currently experiencing prosperity. If we will look and see, listen and hear, what our dreams are showing and telling us, we will be able to position ourselves to prosper in every area of life. A healthy dream life will create a life of blessing and wealth.

Dreams Reveal Unforgiveness and Negative Feelings

Dreams are useful instruments to bring all kind of hurt, negative or the offensive feelings of unforgiveness, resentment and betrayal to the surface.

These dreams permit the dreamer to examine their truly embittered condition. The things they see in their dreams will help them choose whether they will forgive or remain entangled in the prison of unforgiveness. When the forgiveness process is complete, the individual who has caused hurt, sorrow and grief will stop appearing in their dreams. This will permit the dreamer to release the pain once and for all, completing their healing process. Now they are able to move on into a higher realm of spiritual development and grace.

Revelation Knowledge

Revelation is now; it comes to the surface to be revealed as priceless treasures. God has given us spiritual eyes to see revelation so we can become all He has destined us to be. Revelation knowledge of sealed mysteries is revealed to us through trances, angelic visitations, dreams and visions and the enlightened study of God's living Word. We see the same angels, who bow before God, come to us with sacred scrolls and divine messages so both heaven and earth can adore Him. We are called to make God famous. Our eyes see God's glory displayed in new dimensions and behold His expressions because it is the fullness of time. God is revealing things to us that have previously been hidden. Open your eyes and see Jesus, the Beautiful One, full of grace, mercy and love.

Revelation knowledge comes to us through our ability to understand God's written Word, parables, different types of dreams, prayer, and interpreting spiritual and natural symbolism by the Holy Spirit. Receiving revelation from God at night will empower us with new vision. Dreams are filled with symbolic language from our deepest repressed thoughts, feelings and longings. Our personal experiences are expressed in a totally different dream language that requires decoding.

The ancient language of dreams has not only survived from the time man began but now thrives as a universal language. Dream knowledge exceeds the limitations of our comprehension or logical reality by revealing the depths of our being. Dreams dig into the rich wealth of the stored, yet untapped, treasury of resources in our heart to launch them into time. For an in-depth study of how to benefit from understanding God's times, seasons and the watches of the night please avail yourself to all of Dr. Chuck Pierce's published writings on the subject. **Reordering Your Day** available online as an e-book. **Understanding and Embracing the Four Prayer Watches** Revised Version: August, 2006, Copyright 2006 by Dr. Chuck D. Pierce, Glory of Zion International Ministries, Published by Glory of Zion International Ministries, P.O. Box 1601, Denton, TX., 76202 Phone: 940-382-1166, Fax 940-565-9264 Email: info@glory-of-zion.org – Net: www.glory-of-zion.org and three more of Dr. Pierce's books **Interpreting the Times**, **Redeeming the Time**, and **Time to Defeat the Devil** all Published by Charisma

House.

Four Sleep Cycles

There are four specific sleep cycles or watches of the night. We progress from wakefulness to sleep as our known environment fades away being absorbed in a restful state of sleep. Deep sleep will lead us into a rhythmic cycle called REM.

Most dreams take place at night because that is when the majority of us are sleeping. To prepare yourself for sleep begin to still your mind and thoughts. Let your body enter into a calm state of rest by taking a slow leisurely walk reflecting on your love for God. Sit on a porch or in a beautiful garden setting, focusing your thoughts on Jesus. It is important to establish a practice of meditation in the early night hours, around 6:00p.m.. Reflect on the day's activities and allow the Holy Spirit to speak to you in regards to their success or failure. Mediate on the Word of God. Spiritual reflection allows wisdom to enter your heart, increasing godly understanding. What you focus on, read about, listen to or observe will prepare your soul to dream. We are what we see or what we allow to enter our eyes and ears gates. After a couple of hours of peaceful rest (6:00 to 8:00 p.m.), when one enters into sleep, the dreams that occur during the early evening, or 9:00 p.m. time period, contain a lot of the dreamer's imagination but are not fully developed. *"I speak to the Lord evening and morning and at noon; I will share my concerns and speak softly. I tell Him what upsets me and He listens to instruct me! God always hears my voice. He will exchange my troubled soul and give me peace. There are many who battle against me. They fight and strive to defeat me, but God's wisdom has always rescued me and brought me into a safe place. Psalms 55:17–18"* (Author's Paraphrase)

The next watch is from 9:00 p.m. to 12:00 p.m.. When one is awakened during these hours, it is important to offer God thanksgiving. God inhabits the praises of His people. A thankful heart brings multiplication and prosperity to the soul. When we are thankful and good stewards over the little things of life, then God will make us rulers over much. These are the midnight hours in which a person will usually experience a visitation from the Lord or one of His many multitudes of angels. There is much spiritual activity during this watch of the night. One can experience encounters in both the realms of God's revelation light and Satan's dismal occult darkness through nightmares, visitations, and bad dreams. The Lord released the spirit of death to strike and kill the first born in the land of Egypt at midnight. Boaz awoke in the middle of the night to find Ruth resting at his feet. Paul and Silas were singing and praying at midnight when an earthquake shook the foundation of the prison, opening all the cell doors.

Day break is from 12:00 a.m. to 3:00 a.m.. Dreams during this early morning time span are very accurate. The closer a dream takes place to daybreak the more revelation it contains and the more weight should be given to it. A lot of times these dreams will deal with your future. They are a compilation of all the important dream segments of the night, as well as the thoughtful meditations and prayers of the day. This is where the Holy Spirit begins to reveal mysteries and utter hidden things to make them clear.

Morning is considered to be from 3:00 a.m. to 6:00 a.m.. These dreams are from a divine or godly origin and bring the incense of heaven. We are able to gain inspiration from divine revelation outside of the constraints of earthly time. The Holy Spirit can reveal things from the realm of eternity past, present, or future. This is the best time to present yourself before the Lord to hear revelatory instruction, words of wisdom and to gain redemption.

Jesus made it a practice to awaken while it was still dark. He would walk the beach or find a secluded garden place to pray. There is something special and significant about seeking the face of the Lord in the still of the morning's dew, before our mind wanders to the toils of the day. The revelation God brings to our spirit will enhance our total life. The Holy Spirit shows us how to achieve and exceed our greatest potential. The Spirit of truth guides our daily decisions and develops strategies to defeat every destructive spiritual force.

Times and Seasons

During our life we will cycle through many strategic dates and varied seasons. Seasons can last for weeks, months, or years. The length a season lasts varies for different people and for different trials. It depends on how long it takes us agree with God's process, to learn the lesson at hand and respond properly. Each of us has a different life to live and a very strategic race to run. Paul said, *"I'm about to die. My life on earth is coming to an end. My life has been given as an offering to serve God. It is time for me to depart. I have fought the good fight of faith and completed my assigned destiny. I have finished the race. I am ready to receive my prize, the crown of righteousness, which my Lord will reward to me and to all who loved His appearing." (Author's paraphrase)*

For the Apostle Paul, seven was a strategic number. He experienced seven major milestones or life changing events in his life's journey. As Saul he encountered God on the Road to Damascus. He was changed into Paul and he then spent fourteen years in the wilderness as the Holy Spirit taught him of God. It took two complete seasons of seven years each to reprogram Saul's religious mindset. Saul was instantly struck down and blinded in the presence of God. But to become Paul, a servant, motivated by the heart of God it took many devoted years isolated in the wilderness. Paul was taught to discern the voice of God. He learned to see accurately through the vision realm. The Holy Spirit discipled Paul and brought him into alignment with the Apostles Peter and James. Next Paul began to travel with Barnabas. When Barnabas left Paul, Silas joined him. Paul spent time as a prisoner in Jerusalem. Paul was shipwrecked on his way to Rome. And, finally, Paul was in house arrest for two years, where he wrote the Epistles to the church. In all these test and trials Paul rejoiced that he could suffer like Christ. All of our lives will revolve around certain numbers and God ordained seasons.

The Bible instructs us to number or count the days of our life so we may become wise. No matter how many years of life we have been assigned, life passes quickly. No one but the self-existent God knows what a day will hold. No one knows the thoughts of God, except the Spirit of God. The unchanging, omniscient God has given all knowledge and wisdom to Jesus. No one knows Jesus, like God the Father. And no one knows God the Father like Jesus. The only ones who know about the Father are those to whom Jesus chooses to reveal Him to because the Father is inconceivable, unimaginable and beyond knowing. Our God is the God that dwells in a magnificent light no man can approach. Teach us to know You God in the dimensions and manners in which it is possible for a mere human to conceive and experience Your infinite grandeur.

We are fortunate to be numbered among the people who are given eyes to see the revelations of God through dreams and visions. There were plenty of kings and prophets who would have loved to catch a glimpse of the vision realm of today. During their days, the Word of the Lord was rare and visions were infrequent. When God's spoken words are few, there is not power to cast vision, and people perish for lack of godly knowledge. The prophets of old never even heard a whisper compared to the level in which we hear God's beautiful voice today. The experiences and the spiritual realities we have today far exceed those recorded in the Bible.

We are living in the fullness of time, where the former and the latter rains have come together. God has the final Word. His eyes are searching for those whose hearts are totally consumed with a perfect love towards Him. When God finds them, He shows Himself strong on their behalf. He speaks words that enable their vision to grow exceedingly, abundantly above all they have ever asked, thought or imagined in the past. No one dares to say to God, "What are You doing?" But, the wise person simply carries out God's instructions. They obey promptly and accurately, in the right time and prescribed manner.

There is a perfect time for everything under heaven. For the most part, because of our ignorance or lack of understanding God's spiritual language and ways, we usually miss His perfect timing. This is why God has to speak a second and third time, first in one way and then in another. We are spiritually dull, so we have a difficult time discerning God's voice, perceiving His ways and acts. No one but God knows what or when something is going to happen. In God there are no accidents only strategic alignments. Everything and everybody God created in the universe has a specific purpose, meaning and function. Who has sought the face of God to gain the skills necessary to show or tell us the plans and purposes of God? Only the Holy Spirit knows the language of the Spirit of God. We must learn to perceive the language of the Spirit. We have to develop patience. When God is silent He is still mindfully present. God's light will shine at the correct time releasing wisdom to answer our questions about destiny and life purposes.

The realms of the Spirit exist outside of the limitations of natural time; they exist in the dominion of eternity. Therefore, timing is one of the most difficult things to accurately determine in the kingdom of the Spirit. When someone experiences a dream, visitation, or a vision, to them, it is a now, present reality. In the spiritual realm, experiencing the event, feels as if it has already taken place in their life. When God releases revelation, knowledge, or wisdom to a person, from that moment on, the Holy Spirit begins to respond, relate to and treat them, as if the things seen in the dream or vision are already a present reality, because in heaven it already exist as fact. There are actual physical and spiritual changes that have taken place. The sooner we realize that we are a new creation who has been aligned in a higher sphere of God's ways, the faster we can embrace the grand way God is relating to us by the Spirit.

A Life Time of Seasons

"Time is of the essence,"
Is this true?
What will it say of me and you?
Spent well or wasted?
Squandered or tasted?
This time,
This running to and fro,
Can it be captured so,
In a bottle or in a look?
Does time stop
When lost in a book?
A bounty it seems,
A deluge, a heap,
Then a blink or a drop.
Whose is this time?

> Tick, tock,
> Is it mine?
> Or is it not?
> Yes it stops......
> Then starts again,
> Where's the missing block?
> Not lost, but accounted for,
> In the end from the start,
> All the parts,
> Ticks, tocks, stops and starts,
> Seconds, minutes, hours,
> Months, seasons, years run on,
> With questions unanswered for now,
> But this truth stands:
> From dark midnight,
> Till bright noonday,
> My times are in His hands *(Ps. 31:15)*.
> By: Shawn L. Martin

Isaiah tells us, as we wait in the presence of the Lord in prayer, we will gain strength to soar into the heavenly heights to expand the clarity, scope and span of our vision, like that of an eagle. When visionary understanding finally comes to us, we need to write it down to make it plain. Once the vision is written, now we must run to catch up with our proceeding God and His grand plans. God is progressive, He continues on, moving forward waiting for no one. To get in sync with God's perfect timing, we must run to catch up to Him. When perfect alignment comes, our will is no longer separate from God's. Now, we are able to walk in agreement with God, side by side, hand in hand with Him, no longer fainting from doing things in our own natural strength. When we are in total agreement with God, His might will carry us and His grace will sustain us. *"But those who wait on the Lord shall renew their strength; they shall mount up with wings like eagles, they shall run and not be weary, they shall walk and not faint. Isaiah 40:31NKJV"*

Dreams and vision have the ability to change us; the spiritual transformation comes in an instant but the natural adjustments take time to renew our minds and actions. Once we incorporate the changes into our waking lives, God then relates to us as a new creation person. The previous person no longer exists in God's eyes. When the creative gaze of God beholds us; all things become new. The Spirit of God flows wherever He desires and we feel the affects of His movement. No one can control the wind of the Spirit or lock the Holy Spirit in a box. As we learn to submit to the diverse ways of the Lord's grace, His breath, the glance of His eyes, the way He moves, tenderly touches and speaks to us, we will begin to apprehend a higher level of understanding.

Ecclesiastes advises us that there is a correct time for everything under heaven to happen. There is a time to build, cherish and keep; and a time to tear down, destroy and throw away. There is a time to cry, to be sad; and a time to laugh, being full of joy. There is a time to hold on tightly, to nurture and guide; and a time to release others to soar on their own. There is a time to gather stones to build an altar of remembrance; and a time to cast stones away, to forget.

There is a time to live, and a time to die, so no one has the power or ability to keep their spirit from leaving their body at the time of their death. A soldier does not have freedom over his life but must quickly follow his superior's orders. His commanding officer knows the big plan. The leader knows where he needs to move his forces to defeat the enemy. Every soldier has their assigned job, rank and position. In the same way, no one who follows Jesus has a right to their own life. Believers were bought with the supreme price of Jesus' life blood. To live an abundant life we must comply with the commandments in the Bible and the orders issued from the throne with diligence and purpose. Blessings come when we are in the right place, at the right time, to experience the fullness of God's favor and protection in our life's. When the Lord calls us home, at the end of our life's, like Paul, we will be prepared to receive our just reward. If we are faithful, we will hear, "Well done, My friend!" God is a rewarder of those who love Him and diligently serve Him.

God took pleasure in His intimate friend Abraham by directing him to sacrifice Isaac on Mount Moriah. God wanted to reign unchallenged upon the throne of Abraham's heart of love. Abraham was given the time and specific place to make his sacrifice. Mount Moriah is the same mountain on which Solomon built the temple; the identical mountain on which Jesus was crucified. Mount Moriah is a very significant spiritual place, where heaven's eyes have intently watched for centuries.

God had orchestrated the precise timing of everything. By the time Abraham and Isaac had collected the needed material (Isaac carrying the wood) for the sacrifice and made the three-day journey, God had prepared the ram in the thicket. God dispatched and strategically stationed the angels to watch Abraham and wait to see how his heart would respond to the sacrifice God was asking of him. If he was willing and obedient, the angelic assignment was to stop Abraham from taking Isaac's life. Everything was aligned in place. When Abraham raised the knife, ready to plunge it into his only covenant son's heart, God had already provided a sacrifice. He found the reality in the words "Whosoever will lose…for My sake shall find." Abraham found the favor of God as he wholly surrendered his only son in utter obedience. To Abraham if he had lost Isaac, although he owned herds of cattle, camels and sheep; wives and friends it would have been to him as if he had lost everything. Abraham's real treasure was the love he held for God and man. If we pray and are obedient to God's plan and purpose, He will abundantly provide for us too. The Lord who rejoices in song is mighty to save in the midst of His people. God came to seek and to save. Everything we commit to the loving hands of God is safe. God created us to give Him glory. We are meant to see God and draw the light of our life from the beauty of His face.

Moses could not discover the depths of God's glory until he turned aside from his normal desert life path in desperate pursuit of his destiny in God. Moses allowed his spiritual hunger to focus his passionate heart on the burning bush that was not consumed. God, who is a consuming fire, spoke to him there. A casual glance is not enough to search out the revelation knowledge that burns in the eternal consuming fires of God. Total commitment to the kingdom of God gives our hearts access to the concealed mysteries of God.

The Lord knew Moses face to face like an intimate friend. God sent Moses to do powerful miracles before Pharaoh, his officers and all the people in the land of Egypt. Israel never had another prophet like Moses who did as many powerful and amazing things as Moses did for the Israelites to see.

After Moses discovered God at the burning bush, he continued to search for the face of God throughout his life. Whenever Moses went into the tent the Lord spoke with him out of the tall cloud. When Israel saw God's glory cloud at the entrance of the tent, they would bow down at the entrance of their own tents to worship God. This was one of the ways the Lord spoke to Moses face to face like a man speaks with his friend.

When Moses cried out to see God's glorious face, he was directed to a determined place and time on Mount Horeb. God protected him from the magnitude of His infinite glory by hiding him in the cleft of the rock. God sheltered Moses under the shadow of His hand. There under that safe shelter God declared the different attributes and power of His names. God does nothing on earth unless He first reveals His secret counsel to His friends the prophets. Moses saw the back or hinder parts of God pass by as He established His future glory in the beaten, blood, striped back of Jesus. God shared His gracious salvation plan with Moses. As God's manifest presence passed by Moses, God demonstrated His goodness, compassion and glorious redemption of man.

Later, God commanded Moses to go down the mountain and charge the people not to touch Mount Sinai lest they breakthrough to gaze upon the Lord and many perish. God protected mankind when He declared, "No one can see My face and live!" Whatever the cost may be; friends, family, and possessions or length of days; we need to cry out like Moses to see God's glory. Pray that God may grant us eyes that see and whisper truths never dreamed before as He places each of us in the cleft of the Rock Jesus. Let God cover us with His grand hand of mercy that we may know Him in the dimensions of His overwhelming glory. Expect to gain the treasures of darkness and possess the understanding of the hidden riches of the limitless secrets in God.

Moses called all the Israelites together to listen to his instruction, and to learn the laws and rules of God so they could obey. He proclaimed, "*The Lord our God made an agreement with us at Mount Horeb, not with our ancestors. The Lord spoke with you face to face from the fire at that mountain. But you were afraid of the fire. And you did not go up the mountain. So I stood between you and the Lord to tell you what the Lord said.*"

Horeb is the same mountain where Elijah the prophet exited the cave. He had prayed for and experienced the abundance of rain that broke the drought. He felt the mighty wind that fended the rocks. He was shaken as the earth quaked under his feet. He saw the consuming fire descend. After all of this, Elijah moved to stand on the Rock. In this position, Elijah finally entered in and heard the voice of the Lord, and saw His beauty as He passed by. When we learn to stand on the Rock Jesus we will also enter in to hear His voice and behold His beauty.

The dreams and visions God gives us helps direct us to the center of His perfect will and plan. When we are in God's perfect will, all of our needs are met according to His riches in glory. I believe this is why Moses said, "Lord, show me Your glory." Dreams reveal the purposes of God, while visions reveal God Himself to us. Dreams reveal different aspects of our life to us, both good and bad. Dreams and visions should always be interpreted against the backdrop of the Word of God. The Word of God is our plumbline because it is perfect and infallible.

The Ancient of Days is the absolute eternal Spirit whose going forth has been of old and is everlasting. God dwells outside of time in the realm of eternity. God has no beginning, no past or future only an eternal now. God is the great IAM seeing and declaring the end, Omega, from the beginning, Alpha. Eternity lies in the heart of God where the cycle of life never ceases. God is, always has been, and always will be. He was at our beginning and at our end consecutively all at the same time. God has already recorded all of our yesterdays, today and our future tomorrows. The concept of eternity causes man's mind to reach back as far as time allows and to look forward into the future until our imagination is bent and exhausted.

God's love is as measureless as eternity. Time does not pass in God but continually remains constant as a wheel turning within a wheel. Everything that has ever been, is, or will ever be is already within the eternity of God. We are both temporal with an everlasting hope for life in Christ; and at the same time we are eternal beings destined for glory. We were created for eternity but because of the fall we exist in time. Our soul cries out for immortality, so that we can know the eternal God. He has been our dwelling place for all generations. God never waits, yet is patient, nor does He hurry because He is longsuffering. He is perfect always on time. God is not affected by uninterrupted changes because it is impossible for God to change. However, change is necessary for man to be perfected.

When the veils of sin are removed from our faces we see the glory of the Lord as in a mirror. When we see the image of God we are changed into that image from one degree of glory, to the next higher realm of glory, by the Spirit of the Lord. Man experiences redemption through changing from acting like the old man into becoming a new man that is centered in Christ.

In God, nothing happens by chance. He is the Lord, He changes not yet He has an intricate, precise plan, and design for every day of our lives. God knows all things perfectly. He teaches us to number and record our days that we might apply our hearts and gain knowledge and wisdom from the realms of His eternal kingdom. God has never discovered anything. He has never been caught off guard, stood amazed, wondered at something or been surprised no matter what.

Dear Lord,

You know my frame that I am but dust. You have tested me, so You know all about my inborn treachery, even my secret sin. You have created me so You know the way that I will take before I take it. You know when I sit down at Your feet and when I stand up in defiance and question Your goodness. You know my thoughts from afar. You know where I roam and where I dream at night. You show me the way of knowledge and understanding. You know everything I have done and all that I will do. Lord, you know what I want to say, even before I form the words in my heart. I am astounded at what You know; it is too wonderful for me to comprehend. You are all around me— within me, You surround and overshadow me. I feel the touch of Your hand gently resting on my shoulder beckoning me to rest my head on Your chest. Your Spirit goes before and behind me, Your Spirit is everywhere I go under and above me encircling me. I tremble because I cannot escape Your awesome presence. When You have completely tried me I will come forth as pure gold. My times are in Your loving hands. Amen

Time marks the beginning or ending of something. Our days and times begin and end in God. Our day begins at night. The dreams that come on the first four days of the week (Sunday, Monday, Tuesday or Wednesday) usually come to pass more quickly than those that come to us on Thursday or Friday. Dreams that come on Saturday (Sabbath) are usually delayed because they are not as clear, so we may forget most of their content. If the dreamer forgets the setting, details and message of the dream, its fulfillment will be deferred. The parts of the dream that are remembered can be incorporated in prayer to bring about their fulfillment. The sporadic parts of the dreamer's vision that are forgotten indicate their fulfillment will be intermittent.

If the dreamer sees clearly and remembers his dream completely, as if he were awake, it will come to pass sooner. Remember, as a general rule, things that are up close or nearby are seen clearly. Things that are at a great distance away, in time or space, appear gray or blurred and are not seen clearly. The further away the vision appears, the longer it will take to come to pass in one's life.

Dreams tend to concern things that will happen sooner. They can happen that day or the day after; but not in the far off distant future. Dreams are not on the spiritual level that dictates a need for advance notice. However visions are more lucid and clearer, so they usually deal with the distant future. Because of their clarity, they are easy to remember but take longer to fulfill.

The righteous are shown future events in visions well in advance. The greater amount of spiritual perfection and maturity a person possesses, the greater significance the revelation and information that they are shown will carry. The greater the impact a vision contains, a greater moment of time will elapse before its fulfillment. This delay allows time to pray for understanding and wisdom, so the dreamer can prepare for the visions fulfillment, (or cancellation if it's of a negative nature).

The fulfillment of the righteous dreams can be delayed for twenty-two years. Joseph's dream took twenty-two years to fulfill. Joseph was dropped in a pit, sold into slavery, served both in Potiphar's house, and then in prison. Finally, Joseph was brought before Pharaoh to interpret his dreams. There were seven years of plenty, as the dream foretold. His brothers finally came to Egypt two years into the famine to bow before Joseph, making a total of twenty-two years. Dreams can take a long time to come to pass because God has to make the dreamer into the person who can contain the elements shown in the dream.

Jacob honored Joseph, over his brothers, with a colorful robe that represented the different facets of his leadership. The brilliant robe also represented Jacob's love, covering, and protective authority. Joseph was seventeen when God anointed him as a dreamer. (Seventeen is the number of election to walk with God in victory and perfection of spiritual order.) Yet when Joseph shared his two dreams about the sheaves (his brothers), and the sun (Jacob), the moon (mother) and stars (brothers) bowing before him, his father Jacob refused to acknowledge or serve Joseph's destiny dream.

Joseph's dreams were larger than the vision and calling the patriarch Jacob possessed. Jacob, as Joseph's father and covering, could have protected Joseph's dreams. If Jacob had blessed Joseph's dreams, they would have come to pass more quickly. Sadly, Jacob's fear and doubt allowed Joseph's jealous brothers to delay the fulfillment of Joseph's dreams. The family questioned Joseph's call and despised his call to leadership over them. They denied that they would bow before or ever serve Joseph. Their words and actions attempted to change the correct interpretation. Their envious hatred and evil dealings released a curse. Hatred is one of the attributes of murder. The brothers desired to kill Joseph so that they could destroy the dreams of greatness that lived within him.

Joseph's brothers were able to strip him of his coat, but not his visionary anointing or leadership calling. They could not stop him from dreaming God's dreams. God not only made Joseph to rule over his whole clan but also all of Egypt. Once a dream comes, it ignites a creative process that sets destiny in motion. If the enemy can't stop your dream, he will attempt to assassinate your character, like Potiphar's wife did with false accusations. There is always a price to pay to possess the promises of God. The word of the Lord tested and tried Joseph *(Psalms 105:17–21)*. He was thirty when he finally stood before Pharaoh. (Thirty is the number that represents maturity to rule.) Joseph was thirty-nine when his brothers bowed before him, begging for grain. (Thirty-nine is the number that represents dis-ease.) Disease and famine filled the earth.

The wicked are not given much advance notice in dreams because the rebellion and hardness of their heart causes them to resist change. The fulfillment of their dreams usually happens quickly. The Midian dreamed of Gideon destroying their camp, which happened immediately *(Judges 7:13–18)*. The Butler and Baker's dreams were both fulfilled in three days.

Joseph was blessed and prospered in every situation. Joseph was his father's favorite son, the chief overseer in Potiphar's house and he was the respected warden in the king's prison. It is helpful to remember that until someone has a problem, you are unnecessary. Everywhere there is a problem; there is a possibility of future advancement. Wisdom is the ability to recognize opportunities that are generated when an obstacle, mystery, or difficulty presents itself. Joseph discerned the difference in the countenance of the Butler and Baker. He honored them by interpreting their dreams while they were in prison. Two years later, the seeds of honor

Joseph had sown while in prison grew and bore fruit. The honor he showed others provided the door of escape from his bondage of insignificance. Joseph was able to glean a great harvest of favor from Pharaoh.

Until Pharaoh dreamed of a dilemma that no one else could solve, Joseph remained an obscure unknown prisoner. Joseph's gift made room for him to rise to the top. Joseph used his unique, God given endowment of dream interpretation to honor Pharaoh. Joseph provided Pharaoh with the knowledge of how to solve the crisis of worldwide famine through interpreting the coded message of his dream. No one else had the skill or knowledge to solve Pharaoh's problem. Joseph was handsomely rewarded with great authority, power, wealth, honor, and prestige.

The dialogue Joseph held with Pharaoh brought a needed resolution to a looming national calamity. The same conversation also ended Joseph's season of lack. Joseph was appointed as the king's Vizier. If the right questions are asked, a revelatory bond will be formed to interpret the dream. A conversation with the right people, at the right time, will ignite a new season of promotion and possibilities. It is important to be ready at all times to do whatever is needed. Encourage people with great patience and careful teaching; tell them what they need to do when they are doing wrong.

Pharaoh's dreams must have taken place sometime in the morning. The Bible says that Pharaoh awoke troubled in the morning, after he dreamed about the cows. He then fell asleep a second time and dreamed about the stalks of grain. The fulfillments of these two dreams were only delayed for six months. What the dreams revealed began to happen immediately.

Pharaoh asked Joseph to interpret his dream. This created a bond of honor, loyalty and trust between them. Joseph honored Pharaoh by giving him the needed wisdom to avert a national crisis. The problems we face and solve on a daily basis determine our worth and the importance others place upon us. If we are able to discern and understand God's voice in troubled times, national leaders and celebrities will request an audience with us to find God's plan for their success. *(Jeremiah 29:11, 33:3)* When we show people honor, they will shower us with favor. When God's grace and favor rests upon a person, wealth, prosperity, honor, and promotion will always follow them. Problem solvers are always promoted. If you possess a gift, skill, or talent that is rare or unique, you will be highly favored; sought out as a well-paid expert.

Joseph pointed out to Pharaoh the law of doubles; since Pharaoh had dreamed the same message twice, it was established by God. God had determined the things

He had revealed to Pharaoh in his dreams would take place soon. Dreams that occur two and three times in a row or repeat are established. They will happen as soon as an understanding or correct interpretation takes place.

Attar of Nishapur was a Persian Sufi poet, he once told the story of a grand commanding king who gathered all his wise man to demand that they create an inscription on a ring that would make him cheerful when he is miserable and unhappy when he is joyful. The sages crafted a ring with the inscription: "This too shall pass" a possible reference to King Nebuchadnezzar in *Daniel 2:21 "And He changes the times and seasons; He removes kings and sets up kings: He gives wisdom unto the wise, and knowledge to those who have understanding."*

Jewish tradition claims that Solomon was humbled when this Hebrew proverb "Gam Zah Yavur" (this too shall pass) spelled "Gimel, Zayin, Yad" was handed down to Solomon. The Jews have suffered a history of captivity, persecution and holocaust. The rabbi's expanded the significance of the hidden proverb by revealing the meaning of each letter behind this mysterious inscription. The Gimel (3) represented God's mighty acts, His perfect witness and testimony in the entirety of the fullness of His lovingkindness and divine perfection. The Zayin (7) represented the complete, whole fullness of God's protection. The Yad (10) pictures a radical change that had begun to take place in governmental laws and organizations, through trials and testings to bring about divine order and completion in the fullness of time.

Daniel was born as a noble prince of Israel, he was in line to be a king of Judah, but when Babylon conquered Judah, Daniel, a handsome man, was castrated by his captors who carried him off to live in a foreign land. Daniel lost everything yet he retained his honor and spiritual dignity while he served as an ambassador in the court of a pagan king. If King Nebuchadnezzar had not been afflicted with illness, foreign invasions and domestic tribulations, Daniel would have eventually had to return to Judah to transform his Hebrew culture into that of a Babylonian culture.

King Nebuchadnezzar had a series of disturbing dreams. His first disturbing dream of the great statue took place early in the night. The Bible states in *Daniel 2:1*, that his spirit was troubled or disturbed so he could not sleep. His dream was not seen clearly, so he had difficulty remembering it. The fulfillment of this dream did not come to pass for several years. Nebuchadnezzar ordered the slaughter of the Babylonian Wiseman of his kingdom unless they could both tell the dream and its interpretation.

Daniel went home and made the matter of the king's dream known to his companions Hananyah, Misha'el and 'Azaryah. Daniel and his three close friends fasted and prayed that God would reveal not only the dream but also the interpretation to Daniel. Together they asked God for mercy concerning this secret. After Daniel sought the Lord for the meaning of the king's dream, the interpretation came to him during the night. God explained the secrets of Nebuchadnezzar's dream to Daniel in a vision. The essence of what the king's dream revealed was that God was bringing great changes in world governments and the rise and fall of many empires "Gam Zah Yavur (this too shall pass)." No earthly king, kingdom or president is powerful enough to stop the plans of God from taking place.

Daniel praised the God of heaven. He said, "Blessed be God's name forever and ever! Power, might and wisdom belong to Him. He changes the times and seasons. God sets kings in power and He takes their power away. God gives wisdom, knowledge and understanding to people so they become wise. God knows hidden secrets that are hard to understand. Light dwells within Him, so He knows what is in the dark and secret places." Daniel's God given ability to tell the king his dream and also the interpretation saved his three companions and the other sages of Babylon.

Nebuchadnezzar's second alarming, fearful tree dream, which he could recall, came to pass at the end of twelve months *(Daniel 4:4–28)*.

Our hope must be firmly rooted in our love for God alone; having placed everyone and everything else below our feet. To believe in God is to have God established Himself as supreme in every area of our existence. One day we will rule and reign with God, if we endure the sufferings we are going through now. *"If we have died with Him, we will also live with Him. If we endure and persevere, we will also rule and reign with Him if we disown or deny Him, He will also disown and deny us. If we are faithless, He remains faithful, for God cannot disown nor deny Himself."* 2 Timothy 2:11–13

Jesus often left the crowds to cloister Himself with His heavenly Father. Although no one went with Him during these times of solitary venture Jesus knew He was never alone. Jesus was always conscious of Gods' imminent presence. When difficulty, fear and pain surround you, remember you are not alone. God is the same yesterday, today and forever. Visualize yourself on a lush green river bank. View God as an eternal river sovereignly flowing out of your past from one direction; looking straight ahead see the rushing waters carrying your present on every wave; then look ahead to gaze upon the undiminished power of God flowing into your future. Now ask God for His eternal wisdom. Remember weeping may last for the night; but joy comes in the morning. "Gam Zah Yavur" (this too will pass). But more importantly remember the first letters of each word: Gimel – the full lovingkindness of God will (Zayin) develop a protection and defense around you until the (Yad) great governmental changes that God has planned in the fullness of time have come to pass.

Morning dreams are more likely to come to pass quickly because they are clearer and more easily remembered. The closer the dream occurs to daybreak, the sooner it will take place or be fulfilled. Each hour before daybreak usually coincides with a month. For example, dreams at four o'clock in the morning could happen in four months. As a general rule, each of the twelve hours of the day coincides with one of the twelve months of the year in duration.

To obtain a correct interpretation, it is necessary to consider the context of what appears in the dream; then compare it to the dreamer's life and its relevance to their current situation or circumstances. For a dream to be fulfilled, the proper people and precise timing of events must be in position. To help determine the timing of a dream's fulfillment, it is also necessary to determine if the person has the necessary people, financial discipline and support structure around them. Dreams speak of possibilities and future promises provided the dreamer will diligently pray and do the necessary work to bring them into existence.

(See When Will My Dreams Come True? Dream Interpretation Nuggets, Times & Seasons for a comprehensive study on spiritual timing copyright 2011 www.BarbieBreathitt.com).

DREAM INTERPRETER

Chapter 2
Visions of the Night

Visions of the night, unlike dreams, require little interpretation because a voice accompanies them. The dream character delivers the message, spiritual insight or message, an angel or the Holy Spirit interprets the vision while we sleep or as we awake. Normal, everyday pictures or symbols can express the literal values of a person, community or culture. If the action or object appears to be symbolic, they will require more time and effort to determine their proper meaning in the context they are presented.

Dreams and visions empower us to exceed our present natural limitations. We become superhuman and exhibit highly developed qualities that we have not demonstrated in our waking experiences yet. Sleep affords us the time to practice interacting with individuals and observing the various positive reactions or negative outcomes. Since visionary dreams are in the virtual realm and not in a concrete form of reality, we can experiment with different conclusions. Visions allow us to exit the restraints of time. We can revisit the past to experience healing or take a quantum leap into the future to gain glimpses of what is yet to come.

Dream Seer

> Dream Seer,
> What do you see?
> Is it what it seems?
> Wisdom disclosed,
> Plans unfold,
> While dew rests on your branches (Job 29:19),
> Through the night watches.

Peace settles in your Spirit,
Can you hear it?
His voice calling "Open to Me….." (Song of Songs 5:2)
A repentant heart…..
Free of worry and hurry,
Washed anew, a clean slate (Ps. 51:9-10)
On which to write
When sunlight fades
And stars shine bright,
When deep sleep falls…..
The "deeper" appears
In this realm of dreams.
Is it what it seems?
Mysteries, metaphors, and similes,
Parables, word plays, and dark sayings (John 16:25),
Here, where your ears are opened,
Father's heart revealed
And instructions sealed (Job 33:16)
While slumbering on your bed (Job 33:15).
Dream Seer,
What do you see?
A repairing of seams,
A vision of the night (Job 33:15),
A destiny plight,
A renewing of sight,
A restoring of might (Ps. 89:19).
Write the vision,
Dream, oracle, or revelation,
Make it plain,
Then run with it (Hab. 2:2).
Surrender to the running,
Yield to the chasing,
Of this mystery unsealed,
From the dream field.
Faith being your shield,
While your bow ever gaining
New strength in your hand (Job 29:20),
Go, possess your land, Dream Seer (Josh. 1:11)!
By Shawn L. Martin

Each individual must have clarity of who God is in the midst of them in order to align their sights with God's vision for their life, to be progressively changed from glory to glory. Where there is no vision or revelation given by God to guide a nation, the people cast off restraint become lawless and lose self-control. Revelation is not the same as information. Spiritual revelation without a physical manifestation is only information.

There is a governing rule that will keep guard and protect a God given vision. It will bring those who embrace and believe it into becoming the reality of a vision. Where there is no revelation of God's kingdom rule, the people will remain naked and uncovered. The law or tenet of a vision is the principle of the vision. The principle is the main thing the vision demonstrates. It is the plumbline or standard of whatever the vision is showing or revealing. A vision will continue to draw you into itself until you have aligned with what you have seen yourself becoming. *"They made a calf (calf means to revolve or circulate) in Horeb, (Horeb means to lay waste or become desolate through drought) and worshiped the molded image. Thus they changed their glory into the image of an ox that eats grass. They forgot God their Savior, Who had done great things in Egypt, wondrous works in the land of Ham, awesome things by the Red Sea. Therefore He said that He would destroy them, had not Moses His chosen one stood before Him in the breach, to turn away His wrath, lest He destroy them. Psalms 106:19–23 NKJV"*

The children of Israel became like what they beheld and worshiped. They wandered thirty years in the wilderness like a dumb ox. They resembled and took on the same characteristics of what they worshipped. Their sin caused them to fall short of the glory taking on the similitude of an ox that ate grass. They exchanged their glory for that of an idol. They became bound by natural events and limitations. They were dependent on what the earth could give them. They were enslaved, became as an animal, lost like an ox with no hope because they forgot God.

Dream Symbolism

An extensive knowledge of God's symbolic language of dreams and visions is necessary to obtain a correct interpretation. Depending on the interpreter's knowledge of symbolic vocabulary, spiritual maturity and their level of prophetic gifting and understanding of the divine supernatural, dreams can hold multiple layers of both positive and negative meanings. This is why it is so important to search the matter out to find understanding of the dream or vision, *Proverbs 25:2*. It takes wisdom and an ear that is tuned to hear the faint whispers of God's voice to interpret dreams correctly.

Knowing that most people do not compile or record the meanings of their dream symbols, I have created an extensive library of dream symbol cards, which are available at www.BarbieBreathitt.com . The wide ranges of dream card categories I have created contain both the positive and negative meanings of the most frequent symbols that appear in dreams.

The key to interpreting dreams lies in unlocking the meaning of the various symbols. If you know what the symbols represent literally or metaphorically, you can learn the hidden message the dream contains. As the dreamer or visionary unlocks the meaning of each symbol that appeared in their vision of the night they can fit them together like the pieces of a puzzle until a comprehensible representation is seen and the message becomes clear. What was once an ambiguous mystery becomes a powerful picture that brings spiritual guidance and insights full of wisdom.

Interpreting Dreams

Dreams have existed as long as man has been alive. The Roman era placed profound significance on dreams. Lucid dreams were submitted to the Senate for analysis and interpretation. Dreams hold an important place in our lives too. One-third of your life is spent sleeping. In an average lifespan of eighty years, not counting the leap years, the time you spend asleep calculates to 29,200 days. In eight decades you will have spent a total of about twenty-six and a half years dreaming. That is 9,733 days spent in a different sphere! God uses the time we sleep to speak to us. Dreams have the power to remake and transform us into the people God has designed for us to become.

Consider the statement *"All dreams pursue their interpretation."* This exemplifies the creative power of the spoken or written words. Positive creative words that are spoken bring life as sweet as fruit, but poisonous words bring pain, corruption and death. Those who love to talk, use many empty words. Those who listen to their vacant words must be ready to accept, refute, or annul what their weary utterance brings. Diligent prayer is the only vehicle that brings forth an accurate dream interpretation to the point of its development, birth, delivery, and maturation.

There are different types of interpreters. Some learn their techniques, methods and principles from much study in psychology books; but, whose belief systems do they follow and what ungodly philosophies' are they studying? *Job 33:23* advises there is only one in a thousand that is born with the prophetic gift of insight and spiritual imagination from God to correctly interpret dreams. God only shares the mysteries of His heart and angelic presence with those who are His friends, who are wise, and discerning enough to fear His name. God does nothing unless He first reveals His secret counsel to His servants the prophets. When the Lord speaks to a prophet, makes known His plans in a dream, or discloses something of Himself in a vision to a seer, they seek God for spiritual understanding to prophesy His revelation of the future aloud.

The prophetic word the seer speaks creates a vision others can follow. Nothing happens in the earthly realm of existence that has not already transpired in the heavenly realms through the ministry of the Holy Spirit, divine grace of dreams or angelic messengers. Without revelatory vision people cannot prosper so they diminish falling into hopelessness and despair. The greater mystery the vision conceals, the larger measure of spiritual understanding is required to reveal its message. When wisdom and knowledge come they expand the measure of prosperity and influence that follows a person.

People have always desired to know what the future holds. We are insistent upon seeing ahead. But knowing the future can also be a stumbling block to our spiritual advancement if we are not adequately prepared to walk into our future at present. A person's character and level of integrity will form a ceiling that caps their ability to advance. The godlier we are, the more of God's plans and purposes we can contain.

When we place our faith in Christ, He takes responsibility for our eternal progress. He promises to take us by the hand and lead us along a path we do not know, to a place we have never been before. The Holy Spirit will change darkness into light and make the rough places smooth. The Holy Spirit will guide us through the unknown. He will show us the road less traveled so we don't stumble into a ditch. The Holy Spirit will never abandon or forsake us. God encourages us to trust Him to make the crook places straight as we walk through the darkness of this world. God continues to work for us behind the scene in secret, away from man's watchful eyes.

Darkness is not an obstacle to the Father of Light. Darkness was upon the face of the deep when God created the world so He commanded light to shine. God's wisdom diagrams and sculpts our future out of raw materials. The goodness of God insures our highest benefit. The power of God flowing in our lives helps us to carry out His plan so we can achieve our destiny. God is an amazing God. Our eternal hope dwells in the fact that God is good. The dreams God gives us in darkness will direct us into the future with His divine light of strategy and skill.

An interpreter of dreams must determine the purpose God has concealed in the dream. The dream's actual interpretation depends on the symbolic elements and its source; God, soul, and body, good or evil. Dreams remain useless and beyond understanding unless one can interpret the extraordinary metaphors and parabolic forms or find an anointed, skilled interpreter. As the dreamer relates his dream to the interpreter, the interpreter must use their sanctified imagination to accurately visualize the images that are shown and how they fit together in the dream. They must develop their spiritual ears to hear the still small voice of the Holy Spirit as He expresses the purposes of the dream symbols. An interpreter must be sufficiently aware of the dreamer's state of affairs to ask pertinent questions in order to remove the nonsensical symbols and focus in the essential elements those that are relevant and necessary.

Elihu said in *Job 33:14–26*

> *For God may speak in one way, or in another,* (Through prophesy, dream, vision, trances, spoken by Holy Spirit or angels or the written Word) *Yet man does not perceive it.* (Being unskilled in God's symbolic spiritual language) *In a dream, in a vision of the night,* (Absolute prophetic knowledge is given) *When deep sleep falls upon men,* (We receive ordinary, hidden, obscure or commonly known dreams) *While slumbering on their beds,* (Self-induced or occult dreams) *Then He opens the ears of men,* (So they gain spiritual wisdom, knowledge, truth, revelation and understanding) *and seals their instruction.* (God keeps back His strategies for a person's future success until that person's character is prepared and developed to accomplish what is shown with integrity) *In order to turn man from his deed,* (Causes repentance from wrong) *And conceal pride from man,* (Humility will cause prosperity and meekness will create a great inheritance) *He keeps back his soul from the Pit,* (Reveals the enemy's plans of destruction) *and his life from perishing by the sword.* (God's hand of healing, deliverance, discipline, correction and instruction is shown)

From God's omniscient point of view when the dream comes, the Holy Spirit has opened the spiritual realm for our understanding to prosper. But due to our lack of seeking the Holy Spirit for guidance and our limited knowledge of God's ways, His metaphoric language and a working vocabulary of symbolic understanding, the dream remains preserved. Until we seek the matter out, or find a seer or a qualified dream interpreter, our understanding remains unfruitful. Our un-interpreted dream remains just like an unread love letter, sealed. Since we refuse to invest our time, money and efforts to understand God's dream language, He seals up our ability to prosper from the revelation enclosed in the dream so we do not gain from understanding the realms of the future. We remain limited to the boundaries of our present essence.

Without an understanding of our dreams we continue to exist at our current level of natural knowledge. If we refuse to embrace the fundamental character changes the dream calls attention to, God removes our access to the positive actions and strategies He revealed. God seals the strategies revealed in our dreams because of our lack of diligence in pursuing Him. Polls show that more than sixty-five percent of Americans have reported experiencing Déjà vu, "an already happened dream event" or what Job 33 describes as a sealed dream. When a dream is sealed we can no longer follow their instructions to gain God's higher plans for our success. When we seek God with all our heart, we will find Him. When we find God's face, He will direct our paths with His eyes. To increase and prosper, we must love God and trust in God's supreme wisdom, not our own limited understanding.

If we refuse to search a matter out, because we believe dreams are of no value, weird or nonsensical, we invalidate the pictures and words in God's visual message for the sake of our traditions. We live in a time where people want to have their ears tickled; where the clear prophetic word of the Lord is rare and rarer still is the accurate interpretation of dreams and visions. The prophet Isaiah said, *"Be delayed and wait, blind yourselves and be blind; they become drunk, but not with wine, they stagger, but not with strong drink."*

Because of our lack of knowledge in discerning and interpreting spiritual things by divine or prophetic revelation, we are hindered in our spiritual walk and understanding. The lack of spiritual insights and godly pursuits has kept us on the same level as staggering drunks, even when we remain sober. When we don't learn to discern the language of dreams it is just like a blind person trying to navigate the world without the aid of a Seeing Eye dog or a walking stick.

That being said, it is important to note that blind people do dream. Visual images are not the only sensory element that constitutes a dream. Dreams are also full of various noises, verbal intonations, music and sounds. The word dream came from the Middle English word, *dreme* which means "musical joy." The blind person's senses become hypersensitive. Like everyone else, they smell many different aromas and fragrances. They feel with their emotions and their physical tactile abilities. Whether visual images come into view in their dreams depend on whether or not they were blind at birth. Like the heightened senses of the blind person, if we do not learn to listen to, or see God through our dreams, He may or may not show Himself to us in another way. *"For the Lord has poured over you a spirit of deep sleep,* (they are devoid of prophetic understanding or hidden divine insight) *He has shut your eyes, the prophets;* (no perception) *and He has covered your heads, the seers.* (Even those who are gifted by God in dream interpretation will have no understanding of metaphors, riddles and enigmas, visions, or symbolic dreams.)

The entire vision will be to you like the words of a sealed book, which when they give it to the one who is literate, saying, "Please read this," he will say, "I cannot, for it is sealed." Then the book will be given to the one who is illiterate, saying, "Please read this." And he will say, "I cannot read." Then the Lord said, "because this people draw near with their words and honor Me with their lip service, but they remove their hearts far from Me, and their reverence for Me consists of tradition learned by rote, therefore behold, I will once again deal marvelously with this people, wondrously marvelous; and the wisdom of their wise men will perish, and the discernment of their discerning men will be concealed." Woe to those who deeply hide their plans from the Lord, and whose deeds are done in a dark place, and they say, "Who sees us?" or "Who knows us?" You turn things around! Shall the potter be considered as equal with the clay, that what is made would say to its maker, "He did not make me"; or what is formed say to him who formed it, "He has no understanding"? Blessing after discipline, is it not yet just a little while before Lebanon will be turned into a fertile field, and the fertile field will be considered as a forest? On that day the deaf will hear words of a book, and out of their gloom and darkness the eyes of the blind will see." Isaiah 29:9–18NASU

Prophetic or Precognitive Dreams

There are different categories of dreams. There are crystal clear prophetic dreams that often involve angelic activity. Although the angels may not be clearly seen, they whisper God's divine message into the heart of the prophet. These dreams predict future happenings or events that are also called precognitive dreams. Prophetic dreams are valuable tools that help the dreamer build a framework on which to construct a successful future. Prophetic dreams are given to help us prepare ourselves for the future. These dreams offer opportunities to help us positively intervene on behalf of others. Dreams are the doorway into the realms of eternity. Dreams are often road maps that help direct our course, if we will only learn to read them correctly. When we call out to God, our blind eyes are opened and our deaf ears hear a clarion call to fulfill the greatness He has placed within us.

A prophet will dream a dream that shadows his prophetic message. These precognitive dreams leave a strong impression upon the prophet's spirit that transforms the dreamer's life to reflect their prophetic message. Prophets and Seers are gifted to help people understand their dreams especially when it deals with things that have not happened yet. When we choose to believe the interpretive words of the prophetic seer we will prosper. Dreams are an amazing gift from God when they are unwrapped, deciphered and correctly applied to one's life.

Daniel was told by the angel of the Lord to seal up the revelation he had received because it was for another season in time or a future dispensation. Guess what time it is? It is time for the concealed revelation and the mysteries of God to be revealed. We are called to champion God through doing great and mighty works; so a greater level of revelation knowledge, wisdom and truth has been released. If we will take time to pray, seek God with all our heart and look again, things that have been sealed in the past, will be revealed to us in a new vibrant way.

Jacob also encountered the angels of the Lord ascending and descending upon a heavenly ladder. The Lord's face shone upon Jacob as he slept. Jacob beheld the Lord's face at the top of the ladder, overseeing everything that was said and done.

After Jacob served under Laban's harsh deceptive rules the angel of the Lord appeared to Jacob in a dream to give him financial strategies on how to gain wealth and prosperity. It came about at the time when the flock were mating that I, Jacob, lifted up my eyes, looked and saw in a dream, the male goats were only mating with the striped, speckled, and mottled. The angel of God called my name and spoke to me saying, "I am causing this to happen because I have seen all the wrong things Laban has been doing to you. I am causing wealth to come upon you. You will own all the newly born dappled baby goats. I am the God of your father's who came to you at Bethel, and there you made an altar to Me. You anointed the stone altar with olive oil, and made a promise to Me. Now, I am making you ready to leave this country to go back to the country where you were born."

As Jacob left Laban's land to return home to Beersheba, he found himself alone. An angel came and fought and wrestled with him all night. When the man saw the sun was coming up and that he could not conquer Jacob, he touched Jacob's leg and dislocated the joint. Then the man commanded Jacob, "Let me go!" But Jacob responded, "I will not let you go until you bless me." The man asked, "What is your name?" Jacob said, "My name is Jacob." Then the man prophesied, "Your name shall no longer be Jacob but Israel. You have fought with God and with men, and you have won. I have blessed you in this place." Jacob inquired as to the man's name. Jacob named the place Peniel saying, "I have seen God face to face and my life remains secure."

Prophetic dreams are full of the presence of angels who bring us Gd's knowledge, revelatory insights, parabolic imagery and divine inspiration. Prophetic dreams brought astute perception and spiritual guidance to men like righteous Jacob and wise Solomon, wealthy Abraham, Joseph and valiant Daniel, who said, "The Spirit of the Lord fills the world" because every detail is essential. These dreams come to the courageous righteous who are full of God's wisdom. Through prayer God opens the dreamer's understanding to give him divine knowledge of His ways and plans when, like the prodigal son, we say, "I will rise and go to my Father." The spirit of God is always drawing and wooing us to Him. As we sleep and slumber upon our bed at night the Spirit of the Lord beckons us to know God in Spirit and in Truth. *"I sleep but my heart is awake, it is the voice of my beloved that knocks..."* Song of Solomon 5:2

"I sleep but my heart is awake" is an engaging tender phrase of intimacy that relays a romantic depth of desire for spiritual insight. Though she sleeps, her heart continually makes diligent search for her lover. She dreams of hearing the voice of her beloved as she listens for the sound of his knock upon the door of her heart.

The Hebrew word yishenah means to sleep, to replicate or to transform in order to gain understanding of divine revelation. The word "shanah" as in Rosh Hashanah, means to repeat, to do once more or to do over again, a yearly change or another new beginning. In the ancient form of the language shanah communicates the idea of divine revelation that brings change or a new beginning, peace and the power of God. The word shanah is spelled Shin (complete, wholeness of a faithful remnant), Nun (celebration of moving forward in liberty and deliverance) and Hei (the redemptive grace and favor of the presence of God). The word sleep has an esoteric meaning in the idea of God mysteriously completing us or making us whole while we sleep so we can advance with His presence and wisdom upon waking.

If we were to live a total of one hundred and twenty years our physical, natural body would have slept forty of those years or one third of our lives in an unconscious state. Our physical body sleeps while our spirit man remains watchful, awake and very actively attuned to God. God exists outside of linear time because He is eternal, residing simultaneously in the cycles of time; past, present and the future. God shares His revelation knowledge with us while we sleep and dream so we can align our character to gain spiritual insights, prosperity and understandings. This revelation knowledge allows us to redeem the loses of the past, prosper in the present and successfully project where we need to be to thrive in the future before those opportunities even exist or materialize.

God conceals future things from us in symbolism until we have been adequately prepared to receive and carry the full weight of the revelation. Until we have been equipped and transformed in our sleep the dream symbols remain a mystery. But once we have developed our spirit to come into the place of understanding, the mystery is removed and godly wisdom comes to give us access to the promised blessings seen beyond the veil.

Common Ordinary Dreams

There is also obscure, ordinary, commonplace, or regular dreams that are hidden and difficult to understand. These ordinary dreams are given with a weak impression so they are easily forgotten and erased as in the case of Pharaoh's and Nebuchadnezzar's dreams. Anyone, such as Laban, the idol worshipper, and King Abimelech, who had no fear of God, Joseph's Pharaoh and his cupbearer and chief baker, can experience a common dream. Ordinary dreams occur when a person falls into a deep sleep on his own accord, but they need a gifted interpreter to help unlock their dreams meanings.

Occult or False Dreams

The third level of dreams is occult or false dreams, which are strictly forbidden by God. False occult dreams are inspired by the self-efforts of sorcerers or by the choice of a false prophet, or dreamer so they are counterfeit dreams. These dreams are induced by the person's own vain imagination. Their goal is to deceive the weak or maneuver the simple minded or undiscerning people for their own selfish gain. Their dark dreams or trances are induced by various counterfeit means such as drugs, conjuring demons, casting spells or incantations, witchcraft rituals, sorcery, spiritualism, or divination. *"So do not listen to the words of the prophets who speak to you, saying, 'You will not serve the king of Babylon,' for they prophesy a lie to you; for I have not sent them," declares the Lord, "but they prophesy falsely in My name, in order that I may drive you out and that you may perish, you and the prophets who prophesy to you." Jeremiah 27:14–15 NASU*

"Thus says the Lord of hosts, "Do not listen to the words of the prophets who are prophesying to you. They are leading you into futility; they speak a vision of their own imagination, not from the mouth of the Lord." Jeremiah 23:16

False prophets dream dreams that speak out of their own hearts' desires or the soul's realm. Their dreams are formulated from their own twisted, futile imaginations. Their desire is to manipulate, deceive, and control. They operate out of the soulish power of fantasy. They attempt to mold people into following their demands by conforming to their narrow mind, egocentric will or emotional hype.

A false dream will attempt to capture and turn people to serve the dreamer's own selfish craving or aspirations. The vision they cast is void of God's inspiration; for it does not contain His voice. They use veiled words that lead to empty promises and portray false images that are never attained. The false always magnify and glorify themselves as supreme over others. As a harsh task master, they enslave others to serve their selfish wishes and diabolical agenda. But, if there are false men and counterfeit or demonically inspired dreams, there are also the true, real and genuine God given dream. The desire to pursue God always originates in the God who continually holds us in His right hand. If we will continue to seek God with all of our hearts He will continue to lead and guide us into all truth by the Holy Spirit.

DREAM INTERPRETER

Chapter 3
Nightmares

Does your life ever seem like you are trapped in a nightmare? Have you ever had a nightmare that was so frightening that sleep escaped you several nights thereafter, where you were afraid that if you closed your eyes the monsters would return and frighten you again? Have you experienced a nightmare that was so full of horrible images of thick darkness that it struck your pounding heart with dread, filling your nights with terror? These terrifying messages cover us in a blanket of fear. The claws of fear cling to our body with a lethal grip that feels as strong as death. The mind races to catch up with our hammering hearts. Our thoughts are occupied with nervous apprehension and a sinister foreboding engulfs our entire being. The dreamer is bound by a menacing power that is difficult to break for those fleeting moments. It seems like an eternity when one is held in its grips.

The characters that we conjure up in our nightmares are aliens, gangsters, criminals, thieves and robbers, who are breaking in to rob from us, kill us or cause terrible destruction. Our night is spent in a struggling attempt to run from savages, shadows, monsters or ex-lovers who are obsessed with capturing, harming or murdering us.

We walk dark, endless hallways; or we are trapped in a damp, rat and snake infested dungeon. We are ensnared in a dark cave full of bats and no one knows where we are; or we are buried alive in a coffin six feet under with no way of escape. Maniacs, monsters, or a cruel, overbearing boss, tear our emotions to shreds. Who can we trust? We find ourselves being pushed off a jagged cliff, plummeting to our death on sharp rocks. We are drawn out to sea by a tidal wave or swallowed up in an earthquake. Everything in our lives seems to be out of control, falling apart and shaking. Where is the stability? Our own face, or the countenance of our loved one, becomes permanently disfigured by a deep gouging knife, acid dripping on our flesh, or some cruel inhumane torture. The plane we are on crashes and burns or the car we are driving is crushed by a semi-trailer truck, leaving us helplessly locked inside a prison of crushed metal.

Nightmares are distressing to our emotions because they haunt us with the possibility of our worst fears coming into existence. In nightmares, the floodwater overwhelms us; the tornado or hurricane envelop us, transporting us off into parts unknown; we are swallowed alive in quicksand or drowned in a murky alligator filled swamp. We are exhausted, desperately needing a good night's sleep; yet we dread what will happen to us once sleep comes to blanket us.

Description of Nightmares

Nightmares are described as fearful images in our dreams that scare us into action because they are so horrible and painful. The term nightmare was first coined around the 1300's. A mare is the term used for a female horse. The original denotation of the word "nightmare" was a seductive feminine formed spirit who tried to suffocate, overwhelm or weigh people down by sitting on their chest at night while they slept.

A nightmare is a vivid, frightening dream. The panic stricken dreamer awakens with a feeling that the dream is a dreaded reality. They may have a full or partial recall of the horrific dream. These frightening dream experiences tend to occur when the dreamer is processing through an emotional rollercoaster of depression, caught in the cycles of shame or guilt from practicing sin or indulging in iniquity, feelings of insecurity, or they are experiencing mayhem in relationships. When depression is present, the dreamer may ignore pain, experience self-hatred, behave aggressively towards others or retreat into passivity, beating themselves up with self-directed anger, anxiety, while suffering with an inaccurate or faulty memory.

Why Nightmares?

Why do nightmares come? And why do they return night after night until they are confronted? Why is trying to forget or avoid the fiendish creatures contained in a nightmare the wrong response? Why are some people more prone to experience terrorizing nightmares than others? Nightmares, although they are scary, come to bring positive change in the life of the dreamer.

Nightmares teach powerful lessons through pain and the profound things we suffer when we have settled for less than what we are called to deliver in this life.

Every person on the earth has a specific purpose and destiny to accomplish. In some regard, we are all gifted, talented individuals. The more gifts we have been given, the more we are equipped to love God and help others. Living below your potential may be comfortable for a season, but the real you will not rest until you have become the best you possible.

A nightmare can be triggered by the anniversary of a painful event in our lives, such as the death of a loved one. The memories trigger the points of pain we have buried, and all those negative feelings come flooding back to the surface again. These painful feelings do not mean we have not made progress or moved forward toward healing or recovery, but they do let us know we are still in the process. Be patient with yourself. Often people find when a new life chapter is opened or a positive opportunity presents itself, the old will attempt to revisit or maintain its territory, refusing to die. Life is full of different growth cycles that prepare us to develop in time and seasons. When one season ends a new one begins. It is important to glean the wisdom from past experiences and mistakes so you can apply them to the new. The normal response to a nightmare is to run away from it and to avoid it at all cost. But, if you will honor wisdom, look and listen, the past becomes a good teacher for the present. Learning to build a platform with the broken and burned stones from past mistakes will empower us to rise above and escape harmful cycles as we progress higher and higher. Job said, *"For what I fear comes upon me, and what I dread befalls me. "I am not at ease, nor am I quiet, and I am not at rest, but turmoil comes." Job 3:25–26 NASU*

If what Job tells us is true, then the things we fear coming upon us can be empowered to happen to us by our tendency to obsessively focus on the things we fear and dread. Fear is a door we can open or close in our life. If we open the door of fear, all kinds of horrible creatures, thoughts, and feelings and heightened emotions come rushing in to take advantage of us. *"If I say, 'My bed will comfort me, my couch will ease my complaint,' then You frighten me with dreams and terrify me by visions; so that my soul would choose suffocation, death rather than my pains." Job 7:13–15NASU*

What Causes Nightmares?

Everyone experiences an occasional nightmare or bad dream. But, recurring nightmares can work havoc on one's sleep cycles, leading to insomnia and bad health. Nightmares can be caused by physiological or psychological reasons, as well as unforgiveness. If we refuse to forgive people, including ourselves, we place ourselves in the hands of tormentors. When we lie down to sleep, tormentors come to trample all over us. They openly jeer at our faces or use our backs like a playground, or like a street, as they drive us into the ground. Tormentors are legalist. If they have any grounds for their presence they will try to destroy us by saying, "Bow down before us, so we can walk on you."

Stress, anxiety, shame and different forms of fear and sin are responsible for the psychological reasons nightmares come to visit. A nightmare may come just because the dreamer is sleeping in a new location or fell asleep in an awkward or uncomfortable position. A nightmare can be triggered if a person is sick, on medication or has a fever. Also some believe that eating heavy or spicy foods before bed will increase the brain's activity and metabolism, producing a nightmare.

We are the director or producer of our own nightmares. Our subconscious is trying to communicate a clear message to us. Nightmares typically arise out of a fearful, volatile, or emotionally explosive event that has taken place in our waking life. We may have repressed our true feelings and aggressive tendencies instead of expressing our anger or disappointment. When we stuff our pain, anger, shame or any negative feelings, like a volcano, they will eventually erupt, spewing hot emotional lava.

A gentle dream that is ignored will continue to disappear as a vapor, so one continues on their merry way with no changes. Yet eventually that gentle dream transforms into a nightmare that alarms us; shocking us into waking up to some trouble or conflict we have intentionally ignored, disregarded or refused to recognize. We may not be ready to face something we have done or had perpetrated against us or a difficulty in our conscious mind, but our subconscious is more than willing to let us know it is time to face the music. The subconscious lets us know it is time to take the steps to bring a resolution. Nightmares hold the answers to some of life's most difficult questions. But the question remains: Do we have the courage to face and conquer the things we fear?

Ignoring our dreams and the messages they bring will not cause them to disappear. Closing our eyes to or turning away from nightly dreams will cause them to appear in other unpleasant forms. As a matter of fact, some nightmares come because the dreamer has continually disregarded the gentle messages in their night dreams. When the message is ignored, the herald will become louder until they reach a fearful pitch that demands the dreamer's attention. Nightmares capture our interest in a dreadful way. We respect nightmares. We will give them our time and attention because, like pain, we want them to cease.

A nightmare will stop us dead in our tracks because they threaten our emotional wellbeing. A nightmare has the power to deliver a shocking jolt. Nightmares turn us around and send us running in the opposite direction. By listening to, and then confronting controlling sins, negative issues, scary possibilities, or bad habits that appear in our nightmares, we find that nightmares can be used to bring about the long overdue changes in our lives.

A nightmare, like a good salesman, will continue to knock until the door of the dreamer's heart is opened. When the dreamer answers the knock, they should ask the nightmare, "What do you want to say to me?" "What do I need to learn from you, repent of, or change in my life?" "What am I afraid of?" or "What part of my past am I running away from?" or "Who or what situation am I avoiding?" Once the nightmare is confronted and given ear, they will begin to fade when the needed changes are understood, embraced, and addressed in the dreamer's life. Change can be difficult but necessary to remove lack and poverty. If we ask, the Holy Spirit will lead and guide us into all truth and then give us the strength and courage to embrace the grace that is required to prosper in abundance.

Dream interpretation in conjunction with prayer and prophetic life coaching are wonderful ways to determine the cause of distress and then alleviate the nightmares. Often if one's dreams have been ignored for any length of time, a nightmare will arise out of the darkness of neglect. It's like ignoring a person who comes day after day to deliver a vital message only to be refused, rudely mistreated, and turned away. One day that person will lose their temper, explode and just yell their message out at the top of their lungs.

Benefits of Nightmares

Can nightmares be of any benefit? Do they have any redeeming qualities? We have the ability to draw positive or negative things into our lives by simply lending our attention to them. If we focus on fear, we will empower fear to visit or take up its residence in our lives. If we are afraid of someone or something, we give it the power to burrow into our thoughts. Once the seed of fear enters our thoughts it takes root, sprouts and will begin to grow until it takes advantage of us, overshadowing us in our waking and sleeping life. We will begin to fall victim to our own vain imagination, our minds running wild with exaggeration, causing us to flee like a criminal when no man pursues us. Rather than living a fulfilling life, we enter a realm of tortuous existence, groping through a convoluted labyrinth that offers no relief or escape.

What we focus on, or lend our attention to, we empower to grow, take root, and bear similar fruit. This principle will work on both positive and negative things in life. Fear enters our hearts when our minds start imagining some unpleasant or negative thing that someone or something could do to us. The person or situation we fear will take root, grow, and become bigger than life, consuming our every waking and sleeping moments. Fear is an emotional indulgence that brings crippling effects. If we entertain fear, we are inviting a nightmare to reign and rule over us through intimidation. God has not given us a spirit of fear, but a sound mind enabled through the healing power of love.

Whatever we center on we empower. If we plant love, love will take root and flourish in every area of our existence. If we make faith the hub of our life, we will empower the centrality of faith. The measure of faith we possess comes from God to allow us to achieve great works, accomplish impossible tasks, and spiritual feats. If we focus on the messages our positive dreams reveal, they will become wise counselors to us.

Fear has a distinct, repulsive odor that can be sensed or smelled. Fear also has a dismal color that drains our life force or energy; it can be seen on a downcast, depressed countenance. Fear has a specific sound frequency or vibration that can be heard in the spirit realm. The repulsive sound beacons evil and when combined with the odor of fear they act as a transmitter that draws demonic forces to their victim. In the natural fear sounds something like this, "I'm afraid to love again." "No one loves me!" "I hate myself!" "What if…?" "Oh, no! Not again!" "Why does this always happen to me?" "I'm scared to try…!" "But, I don't know…" Fear produces one of the strongest, paralyzing emotions that can be felt. It leaves us frozen in time, hopeless, depressed and despondent.

Levels of fear can be measured through our brain waves and our skyrocketing blood pressure. If we produce the stench, color, feelings and resonance of fear in our lives, we will draw the things we fear and dread, empowering them to manifest and make their home within. By embracing evil, we will continue to push far away from us the very ones who could help us overcome that fear. How do we get rid of fear? Perfect love casts out fear. By getting lost in Father God's love, trusting in His guidance, and choosing to place our cares in His hands, we can remove fear from our lives. Fear has an expectancy of something horrible or dreadful taking place in our lives, while the opposite, faith, brings an anticipated hope that can far surpass our wildest dreams.

From Darkness I Was Taken

Waking to sleep,
Sleeping to wake,
Whose name do I take?
Surely not a name of the dark?
But this monster so near,
Evil I fear,
On bleak anniversaries

Each year...
Dread rising with the moon,
Stars showing their place,
Whose face will appear?
When fear strikes my pillow
And I weep like the willow...
Oh, God, is there one I need to forgive?
To live... *(Matt. 6:15)*
Again?
Waking to sleep,
Sleeping to wake,
Whose name do I take?
Name of the Light!
Restorer of my sight.
A disastrous event,
Oh God, come close to vent,
Your anger on danger *(Job 4:9)*
From ill strangers
Of the past...
A wicked undoing,
Now with kindness in wooing *(Rom. 2:4)*,
Lead me with LIGHT!

Come back SIGHT
To my NIGHT!!
Oh Abba, Papa God, minister
To all that is sinister,
The depraved, the maligned,
Give me signs
And wonders of rescue *(Dan. 6:27)*,
Change my fortune *(Prov. 23:18)*.
Sleeping chamber, fill with glory *(Song of Songs 1:4)*,
Tell the eternal love story,
Make my headboard
A sounding board.
To a new song I awaken *(Zeph. 3:17)*,
From darkness I was taken *(Col. 1:13)*,
Praise God, praise God!
By: Shawn L. Martin

Frequent Nightmares

A nightmare can arise out of many trying situations in life. The culprit can be physical or emotional pain stemming from betrayal, a broken heart, and grief over a great loss or bitter disappointment. Often, when these uninvited changes start to unfold, a nightmare will manifest as the dreamer learns to navigate the unfamiliar.

Nightmares take many forms. They range from the ax-wielding psycho who dismembers or hacks away at the body, to the psychotic scientist who ties us down to his lab table, then injects us with a lethal poison that liquidates our vital organs. In nightmares, we feel our very lifeblood draining from us with no way of escape. A major reoccurring theme in nightmares is the physical harm or destruction of the body. This is a clear indicator that your stress levels are out of control. Your physical body will start to break down or exhibit negative physical symptoms, like bursting into tears, headaches, nausea, nervousness, anxiety attacks, muscle or joint pain, these symptoms will continue, if some type of natural intervention is not immediately incorporated into your life, along with– most importantly of all– finding a spiritual solution. Evaluate your spiritual life and determine if you are doing wrong to yourself or others. Repentance joined with the needed life changes brings a quick resolve to nightmares.

If you are experiencing nightmares, try to institute some stabilizing factors to shore up and bring some needed support mechanisms to help in gaining some positive reinforcement. Avoid making major life-changing decisions until you have reached a more peaceful position in your spirit. Seek spiritual counsel with those you trust and have a history of giving good, sound, wise godly advice. Real comfort comes from God, but we can also learn from those who have experienced success in an area we are just entering. Talking with a trained dream interpreter, trusted friends or family members will enable us to adjust our fear levels. Once our thoughts and attitudes are renewed by the Word, they become like sweet incense ascending to God as an acceptable offering. We will find a source of spiritual hope and an expectation as a positive shift takes place. A simple change in the way we view a situation can relieve the pressure we feel to perform. This will allow the stress levels to return to a more manageable level before we crash and burn. Bad dreams are indicators that things are out of balance in our waking life.

Listen to Your Nightmares

No one wants to be held down in their own bed by an invisible invader. No one wants to be paralyzed by so much fear that they can't breathe, move, speak, or cry out for deliverance. Most people respond to nightmares by waking themselves up out of the dream, only to find it replays night after night, again and again. The good news is that if you will allow the dream to play out in its entirety, without waking yourself out of the dream, the messenger of darkness can be released from his assignment. Once the dreamer has seen the message acted out in their nightmare, the interpretation can come along with the needed repentance and wisdom to facilitate change. If the message is not delivered, the dark messenger will continue to stalk and loom in the shadowy recesses of the mind.

I have found that the more hypersensitive, creative, out-of-the-box artistic types, are more prone to nightmares. These are your brilliant, emotional or imaginative, sensory type people. They can easily connect to others' internal or external feelings or weights just by standing near them. They are empathetic toward or impacted by the feelings or situations others are going through. They are usually good listeners and are able to sympathize with others' pain and disappointments, but they also have a propensity to suffer with depression because they carry the burdens of others on their shoulders. People who have weak boundaries, the fear of man, or allow others to control them through guilt or shame or by giving others the power to make decisions for them, are also prone to nightmares. Any time one's life is out of balance or being controlled by outside forces nightmares will arise to protest. If you are not willing to take responsibility for the decisions and actions concerning your life, you will continue to battle with fear. God gave you one life to live, do not let others dictate your destiny, only God knows who He created you to be. Seek the heart of God and let Him lead you onto a peaceable path.

Fear prevents us from establishing the spiritually tangible boundary of faith in our lives. When a wall of faith is established; the enemy is repelled and rendered helpless. The Bible admonishes us to cast down evil or vain imaginations and every high thing that exalts itself against the knowledge of God, and bringing into captivity every thought to the obedience of Christ, 2 Corinthians 10:5.

Learning to overcome a spirit of fear is very much akin to a workout undertaken by a weight lifter; the more repetitions the weight lifter does, the stronger he will become. God allows adversity in our lives so that we have something to resist. If we do not have adversity, we will be a puny weak person, but when adversity comes and we push against it, knowing that God has our back, thus we grow stronger and stronger. If we shrink back in fear from adversity, we will never grow mightier, giving God the opportunity to celebrate us. It doesn't mean that the Lord won't love us, but we will never become a weapon of war in His hands. He will always rescue us, but if we remain fearful, He will never be able to use us to help Him rescue others. What struck fear in your heart two years ago should not have the same impact on your life today because of your faith is growing. The Old Testament leaders were instructed by God not to take a man to war with them if he had a fearful heart or a spirit of fear, as he could not be trusted to guard his fellow warrior's back in battle.

Your mind is not meant to be given as fodder for demons. But rather the mind is the vineyard of the Holy Spirit, a possession that He inhabits, if you allow Him to take up residence. He longs to keep an ever vigilant watch over us night and day. He takes great pleasure in planting, dressing, pruning, cultivating and protecting our vineyard so it is a place of peace, beauty and fruitfulness.

REM Nightmares

A nightmare is a dream that occurs exclusively during a longer (REM) cycle of sleep. REM is the rapid eye movement phase of sleep. Nightmares usually occur in the middle of the night and last about fifteen or twenty minutes. Interestingly, nightmares are not considered a sleep disorder.

These scary dreams are easy to remember. They carry a profoundly personal message that leaves a powerful imprint. If we can muster the courage to examine our nightmares, they will reveal the hidden fears in our lives. Once these fears are revealed, the dreamer can formulate a plan to overcome the obstacles these fears try to impose. The memory of a nightmare and its restrictions may last for years if the message it brings is not understood and then remedied, it will continue to steal and afflict. By making the necessary changes, fear can be removed from one's life and a new success and liberty will ensue. If one continues to ignore the things they fear, they will not go away, but take root and continue to grow, bearing harmful, restricting fruit that paralyze positive growth and experiences.

Nightmares arouse intense feelings that there is no escape from the monster, evil person, or situation that is causing the dreamer fear, terror, distress, or extreme anxiety. When the fear reaches the panic level the dreamer usually awakens to escape the clutches of the nightmare. If you don't awaken from the dream, it is not really a nightmare but only a bad dream. Nightmares evoke strong, negative emotional responses from the sleeper, which are typically fear and dreadful horror. The recall of negative images produce heightened feelings that may stay with the dreamer for a long period of time. Nightmares contain dangerous life and death situations, with both physiological and psychological terror. Sufferers awaken in a state of distress or great discomfort and may be unable, or too fearful, to return to sleep for prolonged periods of time.

Physical Paralysis

Nightmares are often accompanied by a physical paralysis during the REM cycle called Atonia, a condition characterized by a lack of muscle tone. The sleeper will experience an increased pulse and respiration rate along with more rapid eye movements. While the weight of the nightmare is sitting on your chest, it is very difficult to move. Even though our vocal cords seem to be nonfunctional or lost, if you will begin to simply think the name of Jesus, the Holy Spirit who is always present, will manifest. Remember, only God knows your thoughts; the enemy can observe our physical responses and listen to what we say, but he cannot read our mind. Now, consciously focus on the power of Jesus and His life giving blood, just by thinking the name Jesus and Scriptures from the holy Word of God; faith will arise and the nightmare will begin to loosen its grip. You will be able to shake yourself free from the physical paralysis, breaking fear's clutch by speaking the name of Jesus and receiving the power of His blood.

Facing Your Fears

Running away from a problem never solves anything; it just delays the inevitable. Alice in Wonderland kept telling herself that the monsters in her dreams could not hurt her and she was right! Her mantra became, "It's only a dream; it cannot hurt me!" Eventually Alice was able to draw on the internal courage that dwelt within her. She stepped into her destiny, clothed in the protective armor of self-confidence, to slay the notorious Jabberwockies. The ability to exterminate the fears that chased her was always resident within her. By confronting her fears, Alice was able to rise to the occasion as the brave, capable person she was created to be. Each of us has a frightful monster that chases us for different reasons. Monsters come and monsters go. Our quest needs to be to discover what the monster wants. Why is he manifesting in our dreams? And why is the monster chasing us? When we confront the monster with these questions, we will discover the things we fear. When we confront our fears, we will have the courage to slay and overcome them.

In our dreams we stare at the obvious but cannot see the forest of answers God offers for the trees. Give no room for offense but be willing to endure afflictions, hardships and distresses as servants of a powerful God, clothed in the Word of truth, using the weapons of righteousness to possess all the power that is available in God. As we listen to the gentle holiness and honest love in God's words of truth, our day of help and deliverance from hard, tough, bad times comes. We are able to enter into a wide-open, spacious life. We are delivered from the smallness we feel inside and freed to live largely in God's open expanse. The vastness of God's kingdom authority exudes from us, manifesting in its fullness. Although we live in an unprincipled world that does not fight fair, we do not live a life that is dominated by manipulation, warring against others or exploiting our neighbors through fleshly actions or reactions. Prayer and the divinely gifted tools that God gives us clears the ground of wreckage, demolishes cultural corruption, smashes warped ways of life and wrong speculations, tearing down barriers that are erected against the truth of God. The weapons of our warfare cast down vain imaginations and everything that exalts itself against the knowledge of God. *(See Dream Encounters Symbols Vol. III for a comprehensive list of Spiritual and Military Weapons of War, to use copyright 2010 www.BarbieBreathitt.com.)* These weapons bring down strongholds of impulsive behavior, ungodly emotions and degenerate thoughts. The enemy of the soul is then confined, resulting in our minds being brought into proper alignment for obedience to the Word of God. This results in a godly structure shaped by Christ that constructs spiritual maturity and brings edification to our mind, will and emotions. The enemy of our souls cannot forge any weapon that is able to prosper against the divine power and weapons of God as long as we abide in His presence and under His anointing of love.

Freedom from Nightmares

One of the best treatments to stop nightmares is focused prayer. Ask the Holy Spirit to reveal the root issue that is causing the nightmares. One can break the power of these unclean spirits by using the name of Jesus in prayer and proclaiming the power of His shed blood as weapons against their nightmares. Ask the Lord to search your heart and close any door that is giving the nightmare access. Often harmful spirits come in through fear, trauma, and grief. If we harbor unforgiveness or bitterness against others who have hurt us in the past or present, demons of darkness and destruction are drawn to the dark light of our countenance. Very often, people who choose to walk in this condition will develop symptoms of mental illness, bipolar, sycophantic, arthritis, fibromyalgia or chronic fatigue syndrome. If we do not develop a life of practicing forgiveness, unclean, evil, and tormenting spirits can visit or even take up residence in us. Their curses of mental illness, anger, rage and even murder can be passed down through the sins of our forefathers or be inherited through our generational bloodlines.

The Holy Spirit will help you discern how evil gained entrance to or obtained a toe or foothold in your life. Command the evil spirits to leave in Jesus name. Prayer closes evils door of access, cancels their destructive assignments, and sends them crashing back into darkness. Simply repent for allowing their negative influence. Take a deep breath and breathe the evil spirits out. Ask the Holy Spirit to cleanse, heal and deliver you. Invite the Holy Spirit's presence to make you whole, heal your emotions, filling you with His overflowing love and peace. Now continue to rest in God's pure light.

Spiritual peace and freedom comes when revelation of the truth is received and wisdom is obtained. Major psychological problems, such as emotional conflicts, significant changes in relationships, turmoil, resentment, fear, and jealousy can cause bad dreams. Nightmares often point out what the dreamer is afraid of so those fears can be faced and then defeated. If fear is not resolved and then expelled, it can lead to the manifestation of panic or anxiety attacks.

Panic Attacks

There are a rapidly growing number of people who daily suffer from panic attacks. Pan is the name of a spirit that rests on the chest and throat. It causes a choking sensation, nausea, and shortness of breath, heart attacks, increased pulse rate, dizziness, chest pain, and other negative effects that often lead to depression. Most panic attacks are not caused by dreams, due to the fact they occur in the early sleep stages before REM sleep. Nightmares occur during the later stages of sleep, so we are able to remember their fearful content. Dreamer's who are awakened right after REM sleep, are able to recall their dreams more vividly than those who slept through the night until morning.

Doctors often prescribe prescription drugs, which only serve to mask or dull the manifestation of fear; this does not remove the root cause so the negative issues remain. On occasion, prescribed medications can start a cycle of nightmares as one's body is getting used to the introduction of foreign chemicals. These prescription drugs can also serve as doorways to the demons of fear and panic because fear is a spiritual issue that takes on thousands of different forms and faces. Panic attacks are formed in the subconscious level of the mind. Many different things, imagined issues presumed to be real and traumatic, fearful or negative life events that happen during the day, cause panic attacks.

Nightmares scream their message to get the dreamer's attention. Nightmares point out past traumatic episodes that have been ignored. They can also point to depressing situations and reveal the culprits of stress. When these negative traumas are lodged in a person's subconscious, these entities can begin to take on a personality of their own. These fears begin to self-sabotage relationships and cause a person to stress and isolate themselves from those who can help them. By submitting a series of dreams for interpretation and prophetic consultation the root cause of panic can be found, isolated, repented of and eliminated. A profound message that has been ignored through regular nightly dreams is now heeded. Through focused prayer, and the Word of God, the dreamer will experience deliverance from fear and panic. Life coaching through dream interpretation enables the interpreter to relay the nightmare's message to the dreamer. Through the interpreter administering the right prayers the person can once again take control of their runaway feelings, enjoy life and sleep peacefully once again.

There are two major types of nightmares, REM anxiety dreams and post-traumatic stress nightmares. People who have experienced real life traumas sometimes develop nightmares that are called recurring post-traumatic stress disorder (PTSD) nightmares. The content and imagery of the nightmare closely resembles the traumatic event they experienced in life. These nightmares produce physical symptoms during REM sleep, which include muscle activity, an accelerated heart rate, and respirations. If the root causes of the nightmare, i.e., anger, bitterness or unforgiveness, or occult involvement are not dealt with properly, in total forgiveness of self and the responsible parties, these diseased symptoms can take root and remain in one's body upon waking. The body and mind join in reliving the traumatic event, in hopes of discovering a way of escape or working out a positive outcome in the safe, non-combative environment of sleep. As the dreamer relives the trauma and forgiveness takes place, the dreamer will experience less and less emotional pain and physical impact. He is able to regain control of his confidence each time success is achieved.

To overcome or break this dreadful cycle of recurring nightmares, man devised a technique called imagery rehearsal. With this desensitization technique, the dreamer visualizes an alternative outcome to bring a positive or favorable resolution to the nightmare by developing a different or new ending. They are encouraged to change the bad dream in any way they desire to make it positive and productive. The dreamer writes the new dream down. After facing, confronting, and then removing the fearful parts, the dreamer rehearses a new ending to the nightmare several times during their waking day for a few days. At bedtime, they simply recall the alternate dream outcome should the nightmare recur. The dreamer is able to answer messages or questions the nightmare poses so the nightmare can be released or disappear. Research shows this technique reduces the occurrence of nightmares, distress, and insomnia, and it also improves other daytime PTSD symptoms. This is a good technique but requires a lot of time and concentrated effort. Conversely, it has been my expert opinion and experience that by simply forgiving the individuals who have harmed us in any way, and releasing them from our vengeful desires, brings about a much quicker spiritual deliverance and physical healing.

Dream therapy, life coaching or spiritual counseling is only beneficial if the counselor is full of, and guided by, the Holy Spirit. They must know the Word of God and the true Counselor Jesus Christ personally. By following the direction of the Holy Spirit a spiritually gifted counselor, dream interpreter or life coach will receive words of wisdom and knowledge to set the captive free from the root issues afflicting their life. Rehearsing one's painful past without spiritual deliverance serves only to keep the traumatic violation in the forefront of the mind, exposing the open wound to the enemy and enabling him to essentially exacerbate the offense, deepening and prolonging the trauma. God's answers will lay the axe to the root of the problem, completely removing its negative influence, always bringing a positive conclusion. We can rest assured, knowing that God uses every detail in our lives to work for the good on behalf of those who love Him. God chose us before the world was created, and He has a perfect plan to prosper us. *"But when He, the Spirit of truth, comes, He will guide you into all the truth; for He will not speak on His own initiative, but whatever He hears, He will speak; and He will disclose to you what is to come. "He will glorify Me, for He will take of Mine and will disclose it to you. "All things that the Father has are Mine; therefore I said that He takes of Mine and will disclose it to you." John 16:13–15NASU*

If you want to be totally healed from the effects of the nightmares that come from a traumatic experience, God is the only answer. Prayer changes things. The powerful work of Calvary's cross and the cleansing blood Jesus shed to redeem our sinful natures will deliver, heal, and transform us from all past hurts or trauma. The psyche cannot heal itself. God is the One who promises to remove our fear and give us power, love, and a sound mind. Focus your mind on the things of God that are true, honorable, right, pure and lovely, things that bring a good, excellent, or praise worthy report, and the God of peace will abide with you.

Nightmares in Children

Can you remember a nightmare that plagued you as a child? Most people can recall the torment of their childhood nightmares. Interestingly, toddlers do not dream about themselves, nor do they appear in their own dreams until they are around three or four years of age. So who or what are they most often dreaming about? The world of a toddler is full of new experiences and discoveries that continually expand their horizons. These new encounters can cause a child to develop the fear of the unknown thus bringing on nightmares.

Nightmares strike children much more often than adults. Nightmares are common in children. Normally they ensue around the age of three and continue to crop up until the ages of seven or eight. Children begin to have nightmares when they begin to experience the fear of loss or anxiety that accompanies a new situation. They may be dealing with a bully at school or in the neighborhood. Children, who experience learning difficulties, too much homework or have behavioral problems leading to conflicts with students, their teachers at school, or parents, stress or stiff competition in sports, often have nightmares.

Children are always experiencing something new because of their youth and lack of life experiences. A thunderstorm or the flash of lightening can cause fear. By simply turning off the bedroom light and saying goodnight, the monsters from the closet or those that live under the bed are unleashed. They stagger, crawling out from their dark hiding places, with their distorted tormenting faces and gnashing teeth that devour youngsters. The sound of a barking dog may provoke a werewolf to manifest with exposed fangs and jagged claws flashing. For a child with a growing imagination, the night becomes the enemy that paralyzes them with fear unless they are steered in a positive direction that causes them to overcome the challenge.

If there is constant yelling, arguing, strife, confusion or fighting in the home, a divorce, or a parent begins to date someone new, nightmares may ensue. Divorce, separation or difficulties in the home cause a child to fear abandonment. They do not want to lose the attention of their parent to another. This fear, when instilled, will often follow a person throughout their adult life as well. A major move to a new city or state can trigger nightmares because the child has a fear of not making friends or fitting in. Anything dealing with key changes, an illness or sudden death of a loved one or pet can cause trauma that leads to nightmares.

Another primary conductor of nightmares is watching scary movies or reading occult books, in the vein of the Harry Potter books, or the like, that promote witchcraft, horror, vampires, or monsters of any kind. Nightmares, unlike night terrors, can be recalled afterward and are accompanied by much less anxiety and movement.

After waking from a nightmare, it is important to alleviate the victim's fear by bringing them back in touch with reality. Try to calm their fears and worries, but don't just dismiss them as something that is not real or that can't harm them. Take a moment to write the details of the nightmare in a journal to validate their experience. Explain to them that they are safe and the nightmare cannot physically harm them. Pray *Proverbs 3:24–26* with them to set an atmosphere of peace. Let them know that you will discuss the nightmare with them in the morning's light. Help your child enter back into the land of slumber and rest.

By writing the nightmare down, you have captured the monster for the moment. Pray with them and paint a positive picture of a secure place for your child to enter. Let them know you are there for them. Have them ask the Lord to dispatch His angels to keep watch over them. Teach your child to call on the name of Jesus and to declare the power of His blood to overcome their fear and to dispel the enemy's tactics of intimidation. When a child learns to use these two powerful spiritual weapons successfully, he will stop fearing the night and enjoy taking up his authority and triumphing over fear. Night Terrors

Chapter 4
Night Terrors

Night terrors are different than nightmares. Night terrors typically occur when the dreamer is worn out or exhausted. The dreamer has not gotten enough restful sleep; they continue to push until they are overtired. Other causes of night terrors are drugs, alcohol, fever, and periods of emotional tension, stress, jetlag or personal conflicts. Sometimes, night terrors can be cured by getting several good nights of sleep. It is important to establish a proper bedtime schedule that insures proper sleep cycles. Frequent episodes of night terrors may require someone to wake the dreamer before the time when the terrors usually occur. It is fairly simple to predict their occurrence if one tracks the waking times of their outburst of terror. Simply write down the times of the episodes on a calendar. Then wake the dreamer and pray before the terror demon arrives. This will interrupt the negative sleep cycle and shut the demon's door of access to the person's subconscious.

Night Terrors in Children

Night terrors are not a respecter of persons, it hits young and old alike. Children are also victims of night terrors. About fifteen percent of all children will be prone to night terrors. Children typically experience more night terrors between the ages of two and eight. Night terrors are most common in boys from the age of five to seven. The night terrors may visit for several weeks at a time and then seemingly just disappear.

Symptoms of Night Terrors

Night terrors usually occur between midnight and two o'clock in the morning. When a child is suffering from night terrors, they can appear to be hallucinating or seeing things that are not physically there, because they are discerning a spiritual presence. Their eyes may be wide open, and their pupils can be dilated. They scream hysterically; they are consumed with fear and appear very confused. They may violently thrash about and be unaware of their physical surroundings. Sometimes a parent may find their child sitting or standing up in the middle of their bed.

It is often difficult to comfort a child who is experiencing night terrors. They appear confused, talking and describing the terrible events as if they are awake, but in reality they are still in a partial sleep state. When they are seeing the dark realms of terror, their little heart is pounding at an accelerated rate, accompanied by hyperventilation.

At this point, your child may not recognize you or may even try to fight you in their confused state of terror. I suggest that parents resist the instinct to run in and awaken or comfort their child while they are in the middle of a night terror. This will only prolong the duration of the night terrors in the child. Let your child view every scene of the night terror. This will enable their subconscious to deal with the things they fear. Once the night terror ends and completes its cycle, the child will not be able to recall the dreadful details. The spell of terror may last ten to twenty minutes before normal sleep returns.

When your child awakens from a night terror, they are unable to explain what happened the next morning. They usually have no memory of the event. Children who have night terrors may also experience sleep walking.

Children that are gifted with the discerning of spirits will begin seeing into the invisible spirit realm as a child. They are able to see both God's angels and the evil demonic spirits that appear during the night. They discern both the disembodied horribly ugly demons and the beautiful heavenly angels. When children don't understand how this supernatural gift of the discerning of spirits operates, they want to stop seeing the beings of darkness and attempt to shut their gift down. It is important to explain how divine spiritual gifts operate so they have a working knowledge. Teach them to pray in the name of Jesus. When believers ask God to release angels to stand guard over and to protect them, angels quickly respond by station themselves or making their presence known. Since children are pure in heart, they can see both realms. When angels are present, children gain a supernatural peace, seeing the beautiful angelic beings that surround their bed with light and peace. *(See my book published by Barbie Breathitt Enterprises copyright 2012, GATEWAY TO THE SEER REALM Look Again to See Beyond the Natural for a comprehensive study of the seer gifts.)*

Train your children to use the name of Jesus to drive away evil spirits or negative images from their presence. Teach them to call upon God and ask Him to loose and station angels to stand guard over them with watchful protection. Children can learn to change a nightmare or night terror into a positive experience by using the name of Jesus and the power that is resident in His Word, and shed blood. By exercising their spiritual authority, their faith level will increase and the fear will decrease, until it vanishes completely. The enemy meant to bring fear and intimidation; this can actually be turned to the child's advantage by teaching them to submit their fears to God.

By submitting to God, learning to resist the devil and his plans, terror and fear will flee from their presence. God's Word is spirit and life. It is quick and powerful executing God's plans and purposes. Angels listen and move into action when they hear the Word of the Lord being spoken in faith and authority. You and your child will learn an important principle about God's Word. The Bible states that every time Israel's enemies attacked them, as long as they were walking in submission to God, the end result was that Israel would take new territory. In other words, each time that the devil attacks us when we are walking in submission to God, after we have fought the battle, we will increase in the spirit realm, which ultimately culminates in an enlarging in the natural realm, as well. God has created your child to be more than a conqueror in His name. Your child has an inheritance that God has reserved just for them.

If the parent has a history of night terrors, then chances are this fearful condition or propensity can visit or be inherited by the child. Night terrors run in families until the sins that gave a door of entrance are renounced and closed through prayer. One way to prevent night terrors from being passed onto your children is to pray and break the curse by releasing a blessing. Repent for any generational involvement in the occult realm, such as tarot card reading, voodoo, fortune telling, séance's, palm reading, et cetera, or witchcraft in any form. After doing this, ask God to stop the negative things in one's life from being passed on to the next generation.

Night terrors can also be triggered by reading horror stories, watching scary movies, telling ghost stories, emotional stress, high fevers and by not getting the proper amount of needed sleep. It is so important that we vigilantly guard our eyes and ears, protecting our mind from satanic forces. A night terror is also known as a sleep terror, the technical word is *pavor nocturnus*.

Night terrors are categorized as a sleep disorder called parasomnia. Night terrors are characterized by a person awaking from a deep sleep in extreme terror and a temporary inability to regain full consciousness. Parasomnia happens between sleep stages or during the arousal stage when one is awakening from REM sleep and entering wakefulness or NREM (Non-REM sleep). They typically happen at the beginning of our sleep cycle, within the first few hours, during non-REM sleep (non-rapid eye movement) segment of sleep or in a (non-dream sleep). So technically night terrors are not nightmares or dreams.

A night terror leaves the dreamer with an extreme foreboding and fear. The subject usually awakens with an abrupt or partial awakening, with a scream of terror, gasp, or guttural moans or yelling. They experience tremendous fear, confusion, panic, dilated pupils, profuse sweating, a racing heart, increased blood pressure, and respirations. The person may sit straight up in the bed, thinking they are suffocating. The dreamer doesn't seem to be completely aware of their surroundings. It is very difficult to calm or comfort a victim of night terrors. They don't appear to be totally awake after a night terror but may remain in a glazed, trance-like condition before settling back into sleep.

Most people who experience night terrors are not able to remember the details of the experience; so they are able to return to sleep when a fair amount of comforting and reassurance is offered. At times there may be some vague images of the terrible encounter, but they have a difficult time remembering what it was that scared them, especially if the sleeper returns to a state of sleep without fully awakening.

Night terrors, if not resolved, can lead to sleep walking or other complications. Some report developing a dread of sleep because they fear what they will encounter the dark of the night. Some people recall terrifying hallucinations, where they literally feel snakes or their spiritual eyes see spiders or bugs crawling on them. They report demons coming at night to torment their minds. These demons touch, hit, bite or claw their victims, leaving marks and bruises on their bodies. Victims of night terrors see monsters and demons in the spirit realm. They watch them as they lurk about; sensing evil beings hovering over them while they are helplessly paralyzed.

Night terrors are described as abnormal behaviors or movements, emotions, and perceptions while in a dream-like state, that occur while one is falling asleep, sleeping, between sleep stages, or during arousal from sleep. Night terrors are classified as a "disorder of arousal." Other similar sleep disorders under this category are sleepwalking, teeth grinding, restless leg syndrome and periodic limb movements. Sleep Apnea leads to perplexing tiredness and inefficiency. Three percent of adults suffer from this treatable disorder. Also remember if you are a loud snorer you probably are not dreaming.

Delivered from Night Terrors

An actual account of a person being delivered from night terrors took place at one of my events where I was sharing on the subject of my first book, "Dream Encounters Seeing Your Destiny from God's Perspective". I anointed the whole audience with my fragrant "Dream Encounter" oil and prayed an activation and impartation for them to receive, recall, understand and remember their dreams and visions.

After the ministry session, my hostess introduced me to a fearful, yet beautiful young lady in her teens. She was afraid to receive prayer or the anointing for dreams. She was an intelligent, popular, Christian girl who was also a leader at her high school. She came from an outstanding family with a good reputation in the community. She was experiencing night terrors and desperately wanted them to stop. I took her into the prayer room to hear her story in private.

Angela and some of her friends had gone to a physic in New Orleans to have their fortune read. Shortly after submitting her spirit to the control of this witch, she began to have evil spirits of darkness visit in her bedroom at night. These ominous spirit beings would stand in the corners of her room or loom over her bed at night, glaring and staring at her with hateful eyes of destruction. This demonic network of spies and terrorists had followed her from the witch's den back to her home in Texas. These fiends were on assignment to kill, steal and destroy her life. These encounters with spiritual darkness began to increase in numbers, frequency and strength. Angela's bedroom was no longer a place of safety, peace and comfort but had become a torture chamber of dreadful terror.

She shared that one night a large black door suddenly appeared on her bedroom wall. Her curiosity got the best of her. She got out of bed and stood trembling before the menacing thick, wooden door. It took all of her weight and strength to pull the door open. Once the door cracked open a legion of dark demonic figures began to flood through the unbolted gateway into her room. These bat-winged demons flew at her with their outstretched claws. Other diabolical creatures of the night jumped on her, attaching them to her, they crushed her on the floor with their weight. No matter how hard she wrestled and struggled, she could not break free from their stranglehold. She fought with all her might, but her fist only struck the air passing through their vaporous bodies. When she was totally exhausted; and still unable to free herself from their dreadful hold, she lay helplessly paralyzed with fear on the floor. She was ambushed and buried under a putrid pile of evil.

Months passed, but her fear became so intense she abandoned her bedroom and began to sleep in the living room. Here she would be closer to the comfort of family members. Her mother would find Angela screaming with terror in the middle of the night. At times her mother would have to wrestle with her for over five minutes to get her to awaken from the clutch of the night terrors and the demonic forces that gripped her. Her condition had progressed so far that she was afraid to be left alone. She constantly had to have someone with her at night to be able to sleep.

I shared with her that the Bible forbids people from seeking wisdom, advice, counsel or their future from individuals who operate in the dark psychic realms of witchcraft, incantations, tarot card reading, fortunetelling, *Acts 16:16–18*, occult magic, séances, sorcery or any other forms of divination, *Deuteronomy 18:10–14*. They receive their information from the soul realm, the tree of the knowledge of good and evil, and lying familiar spirits of darkness and demons that peep and mutter.

I made her aware of the Biblical account where King Saul sought out the witch of Endor when the Lord would not answer him by dreams, nor Urim or the prophets. Saul asked the witch to conduct a séance. He solicited her to bring the prophet Samuel up from the holding place to advise him what to do. When Samuel appeared, he told Saul, *"The Lord has departed from you. God has taken the kingdom from your hands and given it to David. You did not obey the voice of the Lord, nor did you execute His fierce wrath upon Amalek; therefore the Lord has stopped communicating with you. The Lord will deliver you, your sons and Israel into the hands of the Philistines. Tomorrow you shall die and be with me." 1 Samuel 28*

Saul paid a high price for seeking guidance from a witch, just as everyone still does today. He lost his kingdom, his authority, his wealth, his life and the lives of his sons. Satan's kingdom of darkness operates on fear, deception, sickness, addiction, death and destruction. Satan is a controlling thief and a liar who will take everything from you, even your very existence. There is no glamour or lasting benefit in entering into a lose-lose situation with darkness. Mark my words, without the help of the Holy Spirit and Jesus you will lose the battle with darkness. Demons and devils do not play fair. It is not a game.

It was my pleasure to share with my new friend that we are destroyed for a lack of knowledge. God did not create her to be a loser but a winner. God would not give her a spirit of fear, but He had given her His power to overcome the fearful things that were troubling her mind through His great love *2 Timothy 1:7*.

She followed me in a simple prayer of repentance for seeking her future in the lies of a fortune telling witch. We followed the lead of Holy Spirit, to shut the door of fear and spiritual darkness. Prayer easily broke the power of the curse, reversing the witch's spells and incantations and cancelled the demonic assignments. The young lady felt light-headed when the spirits of darkness lifted off of her. My captive friend was set free in the powerful name and blood of Jesus. I commanded the diabolical assignment of night terrors to stop in Jesus' name, and they were cancelled. Their door of access was closed and sealed, preventing their return. Then, I released God's blessing over her. A blessing is always stronger than a curse. I decreed the promise of *Proverbs 3:24–26* over her. *"When you lie down, you will not be afraid; when you lie down, your sleep will be sweet. Do not be afraid of sudden fear nor of the onslaught of the wicked when it comes; For the Lord will be your confidence and will keep your foot from being caught."* God's plans are always for our welfare, to prosper us and to insure our success. He is the One who holds our hope for tomorrow and our bright future *Jeremiah 29:11.*

REM Sleep Behavior Disorders

This is the most common Rapid Eye Movement sleep parasomnia in which atonia is absent. Therefore the dreamer is able to act out their dream. These simple to complex motor activities often result in injury. The dreamer my fall out of bed, strike, punch or kick their bed partner, or hit the headboard with their fist. They can suffer lacerations from hitting furniture or the floor. It is not unusual for the dreamer to fracture a bone or to severely hurt themselves.

This disorder may require the dreamer to take some protective measures. Some suggest tethering themselves or building a pillow blockade to prevent their ability to strike their spouse during sleep. If the problem is severe the dreamer may have to resort to placing their mattress on the floor in the center of an empty room. The best solution is to prayerfully seek deliverance and healing from this disorder or any other negative spiritual condition. The powerful name of Jesus is above every name so when the Holy Spirit is invited in, He takes over and every disorder must move out.

Characteristics of RBD

Most (90%) of the REM Behavior Disorder (RBD) victims are males over fifty years of age. The most common age for the onset of this disorder is from fifty to sixty-five. But RBD can begin as young as twenty and extend until the ripe old age of eighty. It may be accompanied by an outburst of swearing, screaming, or simply talking in their sleep. This disorder may be associated with neurodegenerative disease such as Parkinson's disease, multiple system atrophy or dementia. People who suffer from narcolepsy are more prone to develop RBD. The onset of this disorder can also be the result of side-effects to prescribed medications, such as antidepressants. This is why it is always best to remedy spiritual disorders through the leading of the Holy Spirit and not through consuming another drug cocktail.

Confusional Arousal Disorder

Confusional arousal is another form of sleep disorders. When someone suffers from an episode of confusional arousal, they awaken in a disoriented, bewildered and agitated, frantic state. This state of confusion may last anywhere from 3 to 30 minutes. They may strike out at people or flay at invisible things or spirits, sob, moan or engage in aggressive, confrontational behavior.

Arousal disorders, such as sleepwalking and night terrors, occur when a person is experiencing problems transitioning through the different phases of sleep. The brain sends two conflicting messages to the body. The major muscle groups of the body are still paralyzed, as if they are in deep sleep, but the brain is also sending messages and images to the person that they are awake. This causes an altered state of consciousness. Dissociation takes place when the brain communicates two opposite states at once, as when a person is lucid dreaming. Lucid dreaming is when a person is asleep, but they know they are dreaming. People who suffer from night terrors, confusional arousal or sleepwalking have a difficult time reaching or remaining in a deep sleep phase.

Chapter 5
Sleepwalking

Sleepwalking is a sleep disorder in the parasomnia family. It is prevalent in one to fifteen percent of the population. Sleepwalking is also known as somnambulism. It is more prevalent in children and usually begins to disappear during adolescence. Adult sleepwalking is rarer. Sleepwalkers move about during their low sleep stage. They are able to perform feats that are usually done during a wakeful state of consciousness. These activities vary depending upon the person. They may simply sit up in bed, straighten their nightstand, or walk to the bathroom. In extreme cases the sleepwalker may attempt to drive a car, violently strike someone or even attempt murder. Since sleepwalkers are not conscious, they usually have no memory of their escapades. Their glazed eyes are open as if awake. The sleepwalker may move about for thirty seconds to thirty minutes at a time.

Causes of Sleepwalking

Sleepwalking can also be caused by certain prescribed medications. These medications come with pharmaceutical warnings of patients reportedly having walked around their homes, plundering through their refrigerators, eating a meal and even driving their vehicles, all without any recollection of having done so the following day. Some theorize that sleepwalking may develop in children due to a maturity delay in the central nervous system. Children can inherit sleepwalking disorders if one or both of their parents are or were sleepwalkers. Sleepwalking is a common event for twenty percent of children between the ages of four to eight. During these young formative years children may also experience nocturnal enuresis or bedwetting. I can remember experiencing bedwetting as a child. I would think I was awake. I would sit up in bed and look around. I would feel for the toilet, the bathroom walls, and the toilet paper roll. I assured myself I was definitely in the bathroom this time. Yet, I was still in bed. In the morning I would discover I had once again wet my bed.

Treatments of Sleepwalking

Sleepwalking and other physical and mental disorders may also have a negative spiritual root, especially if the person has naively or intentionally submitted themselves to a hypnotist, Scientologist, the occult or New Age healers. Often unbeknown to the seeker, demonic spirits are introduced by a person who is involved in occult practices and unclean spirits take up residence in that person. Hypnotist, Swami's, Christian Scientist and New Age healers do not heal people; they merely shift demonic presences around. They expel a lesser demon or cause it to become dormant as a stronger more deadly spirit is conjured up, introduced and given entrance into the person. Later these same spirits will manifest their will and desires, emit sickness or their type of disease through the body of the person they inhabit. Deliverance in the name of Jesus is needed to expel these unwanted demonic guests. The name of Jesus is the only name that is above every other named spirit or disease. When the person is set free from demonic spirits they may then resume control of their life and regain the mental and physical health of their body.

It is important to get plenty of sleep and stay rested so our spirit remains strong and alert. Some doctors prescribe drugs for sleepwalkers, but this opens a door of access for other spirits. It is recommended that sharp objects or dangerous items be removed from the sleepwalker's environment. Locked doors and windows will also help to limit their roaming range. Some feel one should guide the sleepwalker back to bed without waking them, to avoid causing confusion or disorientation. The best treatment that I could prescribe is covering the oppressed person with the blood of Jesus, praying anointed healing prayers, along with a powerful deliverance by casting out the demons that are haunting them in the name and power of Jesus Christ.

Counting Sheep.....Will I Ever Sleep?

Counting sheep,
Off to sleep…..
But my bed brings no comfort (Job 7:13).
Instead nightmares and terrors,
With hairy creatures,
And scary features,
In my dreams appear.
From deep sleep I am shaken,
My precious rest taken.
Punching pillows,
Hitting the floor,
Let me out!
Where is the door?
Counting sheep,
Finally back to sleep…..
Will my couch ease my complaint (Job 7:13)?
Though life is preserved for a saint (Ps. 97:10),
It seems I've drowned,
Can't make a sound.
Running through the night,
Filled with fright,
Hallways, dungeons, rats,
Forests, caves, and bats,
The car's in reverse,
Coffin in a hearse,
Suffocation, death, pain,
Stripped, naked, and ashamed,
Blown by wind, gust and gale,
Choked till I'm pale,
Plunging off a cliff,
Scared stiff,
Is this real or myth?
Counting sheep,
Will I ever sleep?
Heart pounding,
Screams resounding,
Gators and traitors,
Where's my Creator?
Is He truly greater

Than what looms in my dreams?
I'm torn at the seams (Job 17:11).
Shakes, snakes and toothaches,
Nothing happens when I step on the brakes!!!
Is this real or fake?
Which direction do I take?
What happens when I wake?
Blood, cuts and bruises,
Can't win for losing,
On and on, every night,
No end in sight,
Waking in a sweat,
With horrendous evil I am beset,
When will help arrive?
Will I truly survive?
This terror of the dark,
Which grips my heart?
By: Shawn L. Martin

Wet Dreams

Dream research has proven that brain waves are more energetic at night when dreaming than when awake. Females are more verbal and dream more often than males; even through the male is considered to be more visually stimulated. Physiological researchers have found that during dreaming REM sleep, males experience erections and females experience increased vaginal blood flow, regardless of the content of the dream. In fact, "wet dreams" may not necessarily correspond with explicitly sexual dream content. It is very normal for males to experience an erection during the REM stage of sleep, even when they are not dreaming anything of a sexual nature.

A beautiful woman in her twenties, who has escaped the traumatic trap of the sex trade industry, shared her experience with me. She told of a gory, grotesque demonic presence that appeared as a half man, half woman spirit, which would come to her at night while she was awake. This naked spirit would try to seduce her into having sex, begging her to come back to her life of sexual abuse and perversion. God's love removed her blinders, and His mercy showed her the truth of how ugly this seductive perverse spirit really looked. She is still free today and helping others get free from this sexually diabolical entrapment. At times a demonic spirit called a Lilin (a disease bearing wind), a night spirit, or an incubus or succubus spirit, may also be involved in producing terrors, nightmares, unclean or sexually perverted dreams.

The marriage bed is holy and undefiled. Anything that does not violate a person's moral integrity, which is agreed upon between a married man and wife, is considered appropriate. Sexual relations between a married man and woman is one of the most beautiful gifts God has given a couple to express their intimate love to one another. Additionally, intercourse is the way a husband and wife become fruitful and reproduce themselves in the next generation. However, if you are not married and your dreams are filled with sexual escapades your carnal nature or a spirit of lust is most likely ruling your decisions. Consider what type of images or movies you are watching. Scripture uses allegories, symbols, types and parables to depict sexual immorality, promiscuity, perversion or unfaithfulness and dreams will use the same type of imagery to communicate a clear message.

Sexual dreams can be a call to experience a greater measure of intimacy with God or others. Sex dreams can be a warning that unclean thoughts or attitudes will lead to immoral acts if repentance doesn't take place. Aside from this, sexual relations as experienced in a dream can be an invitation for the dreamer to join hands or forces with an outside group, organization, church, business or person.

Society has made sex into a god that is worshipped. Sex dreams can leave you feeling refreshed, loved and productive when they are of God. But when their source is not of God but of the lust of the flesh or a spirit of perversion, it leaves the dreamer feeling dirty, defiled and unclean. When dreaming, are your sexual partners the same or opposite sex? Same sex partners indicate a type of perversion that prevents reproduction from taking place, insuring the couple will not carry on into the next generation. This type of dream indicates your relationship will not be fruitful but come to a dead end. A lot of people only develop relationships with people who have embraced their same philosophies or agree with their belief systems. Although this type of relationship may seem to be peaceable it is very sterile and nonproductive. Opposites attract which adds an explosive element and iron sharpens iron when two conflicting opinions or sexes emerge together as one.

In your dream, are you engaging with an old flame from the past or igniting a new love relationship? The former or current people that you find yourself entangled with will indicate where your passions lie. When we adore someone and allow our hearts to idolize them we often place them on a pedestal above God. To experience true intimacy in the marriage bed the clothes are removed. In dreams being naked is a symbol that one needs to be transparent, open, remove the mask to become vulnerable, open and honest. (Refer to my *Dream Sexology* symbol book copyrighted 2010 on www.BarbieBreathitt.com for a better understanding of how these spirits operate.)

DREAM INTERPRETER

Chapter 6
Animals & Creatures Great and Small

The animals that appear in our dreams have significance. Some animals we love and are easily drawn to while others we fear and run from. When an animal appears in a dream, the dreamer should ask the following questions: Are the animals that appear domestic, family pets, extinct, tamed or wild? What characteristics, attributes or functions do they perform? Do I like and feel positively toward the animal, or do I dislike and feel negatively toward them? Does this animal appear in the Bible, and, if so, in what context? The animals that visit our dreams can have direct correlation to the way we are acting or behaving in our lives.

God is our architect and He is also the creator of the animal kingdom. God's accuracy in dreams and attention to details in the creation of the world can be observed in the hatching of eggs. Have you ever noticed that the number of days it takes to incubate and hatch an egg is divisible by seven, the number of days in a week? For example the eggs of the potato bug hatch in 7 days; those of the canary in 14 days; those of the barnyard hen in 21 days; the eggs of ducks and geese hatch in 28 days; those of the mallard duck hatch in 35 days. The eggs of the little parrot and the big ostrich hatch in 42 days.

God's creative genius is seen in the making of an enormous elephant. God planned that this beast would have a huge body, a long trunk, short tail and would be too large to bear on two legs. The four legs of this great animal all bend forward in the same direction. No other quadruped is so made. For this reason God gave the elephant four adjustable fulcrums so that it can easily raise its massive body from the ground. The horse rises from the ground on its two front legs first. A cow rises from the ground with its two hind legs first. How wise the Lord is in all His works of creation!

(See Dream Encounters Symbols Vol. I for a comprehensive list of Dream Symbol cards on Animals, Creatures Great and Creatures Small, to use copyright 2010 www.BarbieBreathitt.com).

Monster Mania

When dreaming consider the attributes of the animals or the animalistic monster or the characteristics of the dangerous person who is pursuing you. What type of animal appears in your nightmare? Do they represent your wild or untamed self? Does your own personality possess any of the same traits? Do you feel out of control, threatened or overpowered? Who is the stranger that is lurking in the shadows? Is it you? Are you intentionally hiding from your dark or mysterious side? Are you afraid to be open and vulnerable with your true feelings towards someone? Are you troubled with feelings of rejection? Are you scared to love again? Maybe you are afraid that if you allow yourself to express your feelings to someone they will break your heart? Are you holding back so you will not experience the pain of rejection?

Running away from a problem never brings a resolution. The problem will not disappear just by choosing to ignore it or telling yourself it doesn't exist. The problem will remain until you take control of your emotions and turn yourself around. You must position yourself in a place of courage to face the monster in order to overcome the problem. If you continue to retreat and run away, the animalistic monster will continue to chase you. These dreams indicate there are issues in your life that need attention. Changes need to be made.

Examine the dream. Who is chasing you? Why are you running? Are you running away from your destiny or a higher calling? Are you running away from responsibility? Are you trying to avoid using the authority you have been given? Are you afraid of making a mistake? Confrontation is never easy, but it is necessary for growth. Look at the dream as a whole. What is its message? If there is something or someone trying to prevent you from taking the next step or moving into a higher place of success, remove it by facing it.

Chapter 7
Body Dreams

Each one of us is fearfully and wonderfully created as individuals to reflect the beauty of our Creator. There are not any two people who are exactly the same. God has engineered our bodies to function in an amazing way. Each organ has a specific color and function that joins with the body's other systems to communicate messages carried from the brain. Your body lets you know when you are tired, hungry, and thirsty or lacking specific vitamins, nutrients or minerals. It will also let you know when there is something wrong with your body or soul.

Your body is able to communicate to you through the realm of dreams. If one pays close attention to their dream symbols, their body will begin to tell them everything they need to do to be healthy and happy in life. The images of one's body in a dream will speak to your potential, your wellbeing and it will also speak to present circumstances that are negatively affecting your health. By learning to listen to what your dreams are telling you one can prevent or preempt disease in its beginning stages. Simply observe the parts of the body that are shown in a dream. This will allow the dreamer to place small clues together to discover wisdom and needed insights about their body.

When my body is dehydrated I dream of going to the kitchen at night to drink large amounts of 7UP or iced tea. I see myself standing before the refrigerator door just drinking the whole bottle down. The 7UP dream symbol is a signal that tells me something is UP, or wake up to drink more fluids during the day. Seven is a number that means completeness, wholeness, fullness, spiritual perfection and development, purification and consecration; so when that number appears in my dream, I know I am lacking something. In this case I need to fill my body up with fluids. When I dream of ice tea I am reminded of the Nestea commercial of the person plunging into the pool of water with their glass full of tea. I know I need to refresh my body with fluids.

Our bodies are so fine-tuned that they are able to communicate to us, through a symbolic dream language at night, the specific minerals, vitamins, food, or fluid we need. Each of our organs is a different color so they require different vitamins to keep them healthy and functioning to their fullest potential and potency. If my body is low on potassium, niacin, or calcium, I will dream of climbing a banana tree. If I don't eat some bananas in the next few days, I will awaken at night with severe leg cramps in my calves. Pain is a good teacher. I'd much rather eat bananas or take my vitamins when my body tells me to. In dreams bananas represent a gentle person who opens up to people very easily to share the softness of their sweet insides.

In dreams our body represents our life or who we are. It is the physical house that holds our spirit and our soul. If we don't take care of our physical body, the rest of us, our emotional and spiritual life will not prosper. There are so many things that can cause our bodies to fail or become weak. Sin, unforgiveness, shame and guilt, worry, fear, anxiety, disappointment and heartbreak, overeating, drugs and alcohol, stress and anger just to name a few, can really work a number on our bodies. If not dealt with properly and removed from our lifestyle, any one or combination of these detractors will cause your body to age, develop disease or shut down prematurely. We were not created to carry these negative forces in our daily life. This is why it is so important to keep short records of wrongs done to us and embrace a lifestyle of forgiveness and extend grace to others quickly.

Feet

In dreams our bodies will often highlight, magnify or feature different body parts. When that part of the body comes to the forefront in a dream, it is important to ask yourself why? What is the function of that particular body part? For example, feet are often seen in dreams. Sometimes the feet are bare, which can mean the person is unprepared, ill equipped or vulnerable to outside elements. Feet can also represent a messenger or bearer of good news who is coming with hope and salvation, so their feet appear beautiful in the dream. "How beautiful are the feet of those who bring good news of excellent things!" If the feet are bare it can refer to us being in a situation like Moses, who was asked to remove his sandals because he was standing on holy ground. Yet more often than not, bare feet represent someone who is handicapped, vulnerable, not shod, or prepared properly so they are at a disadvantage or not equipped for their passage. Bare feet indicate there are obstacles that will need to be overcome to advance. Their forward progress can be easily hindered by offenses or social prejudices. Of course, being a third generation native Floridian by birth, I enjoy going barefooted as much as possible. To me it is so natural to go barefoot, it represents ease, comfort and being relaxed, or at home. I love to walk the beach in my bare feet.

Then other times feet have on tennis shoes, dress shoes, Cinderella glass slippers, or Stella heels or you see your mother wearing army boots. The various types of shoes that clothe our feet will represent the roles we are taking on in life. The shoes we are wearing can also represent an inner conflict between the way we are at present and the person we desire to become.

What do the different actions feet take mean or represent? We stand, walk and run on our feet. Feet represent our ability to move from one place to another. Our feet are foundational in that they give us support and often represent our decision-making ability. Feet represent the foundational issues in life, to be well or poorly grounded in life, to have one's feet planted solidly on the ground. Feet can lead us into trouble or enable us to walk away from temptation. When our feet are shod with the preparation of the gospel of peace, feet can tread on a serpent, on accusations, or we can place our enemy's lies under our feet as a building or stepping stone to our next level of character development.

Are we going to use our feet to climb on top of others? Or will we use our feet to help carry a friend or even an enemy to a place of safety? Our feet can represent our natural or our spiritual walk in life. If we are digging our heels in, or resisting movement, we could be allowing our stubborn nature to rule or we may be fearful of taking the next step in our relationship or job.

Feet that kick or strike out speak of someone who is rebelling against authority or feels they are losing control of their own ability to make decisions. Feet that are lame or diseased can represent a lack of faith, a skeptic who is walking in error, unbelief or doubt. This person's walk can also be affected by situations they have not forgiven, so an attitude of bitterness is developing.

If one's feet are itching or heating up in a dream, then travel or changes are coming. To bathe someone else's feet is an act of humility or represents washing away fear that may be hindering forward movement. If the feet are aching in one's dream, it can indicate troubles in relationships. Dirty feet are a warning to guard one's reputation by staying out of questionable areas; keep your feet on the narrow path that leads to life. If the feet are cold this warns of disappointment or fear. If the foot is broken one can expect foul play, loss, sickness or obstacles.

Growths or Wounds

Growths can signify something harmful that is present and growing in our lives that should not be. Warts, cancers, tumors, cyst, and lumps or bumps let us know there is a negative psychological or emotional reaction that is quickly forming that needs our attention. It is important that the dreamer focuses on this negative growth pattern in their life to bring it to a resolve, seek counseling, or forgiveness so that a root of bitterness doesn't spring up and defile everyone who is involved or associated with the problem. It is important to bring the necessary changes and not just cope with a chronic problem that will only continue to grow with time.

Burns, Lacerations or Scrapes, Scratches and Scars

Burns, lacerations or scrapes on the skin or certain body parts let the dreamer know they have been through a very difficult situation, a narrow escape or a close call. They may have been burned in a romantic entanglement and they have come out of that relationship with their feelings being seared.

Some people who receive third degree burns never recover. They are afraid to love or feel again. They won't allow anyone close enough to touch them again. Their significant other, mate, or maybe their boss, or close friend has lashed out at them with verbal abuse or accusing words. These hurtful words and devastating situations could have developed into a divorce or in the person being fired.

Scrapes usually indicate one has fallen down on their journey or were tripped up by someone who opposed or rejected their advances. At any rate they barely scraped by and they are left with the scars to prove it. The deeper, wider, and more pronounced the wound, the deeper the emotional pain. The worse the laceration, the longer amount of time it will require for a total healing to take place.

Scratches usually indicate an altercation with women since they are more prone to strike out with their fingernails. More women are accustomed to maintaining a bi-weekly nail appointment or what we call a manicure. When nails are used to produce scratches in a dream it can indicate there is a requirement for healing, restoration, or a cure with a woman and man situation, a man-i-cure is needed.

Scars represent emotional trauma or physical abuse, pain being inflicted, a mistake or sin leaving its mark, so the dreamer is in need of forgiveness or healing. Men's dreams revolve around competing with other men, while women dream equally about both men and women.

Losing Limbs

Today the divorce rate is escalating. It doesn't seem to matter whether the couples are believers or non-believers. We see divorce taking its toll on both newly wed and those who have been together for decades. When people experience the level of pain this magnitude of separation generates, they will often dream of losing major parts of their body. The dreamers will see themselves as a living sacrifice. Their bare chest is being bent over a primitive stone altar, while their mate holds a curved blade waiting to plummet it into their ribs, to cut out their bleeding heart. In other dreams their head is cut off on a chopping block while their hands are securely tied behind their back, rendering them a helpless victim. Life is full of choices, but if we compromise our principles, our dreams will reflect those severe sacrificial compromises as wounds. No one is worth you totally sacrificing or losing sight of yourself or forfeiting your long-term happiness over, due to divorce. There is life after divorce.

Legs

Legs carry us through difficult situations; they empower us to make a stand. Legs enable us to walk through life. Our legs are our support system and motivation. Women's legs represent grace, beauty, and enticement. If a leg is cut off or amputated, it can mean financial ruin, loss of friends, or unbearable grief at home. We lose our leg in dreams when we are trying to mold our life to fit a new love relationship or we are trying to maintain some type of emotional balance during a painful break up.

If you are having surgery to attach a new leg to your body, you may have just become engaged or moved in with your significant other without getting married. You may be questioning your decision and wondering how you are going to stand or be properly balanced with three legs. You are still attempting to locate yourself in all these changes and bring some type of equilibrium to your new walk in life. Remember, no one has three legs in real life. This dream is warning you that living with someone without being married to them, will place you at a great disadvantage. You are freely giving of yourself with no covenant security or guarantees. You are setting yourself up for heartbreak, disappointment, rejection and great loss. If he or she really loves you, they will commit to marrying you. If they just want to try things out, tell them that you are not interested in a trial run, that you are very special, a highly valued jewel in the sight of God, and that you are not interested in devaluing or degrading yourself, but have decided to take a step back and wait for God's best for you.

Broken Hearted or Breakthrough?

God is not a respecter of persons but is God's love unique to those who have suffered a wounded heart? Does the Holy Spirit only bring comfort during the times of our brokenness? The Bible tells us that, *"The Lord is near to the brokenhearted (shabar: the fractured, ruined, the crushed, torn, destroyed, broken through destruction, breakthrough) and saves those who are contrite (crushed, mutilated, beaten to pieces, or wounded to the point of physical or mental collapse) in spirit." Psalms 34:18*

Hebrew words can be ambiguous which allows one word the freedom to paint many different pictures. Another interpretation for *shabar (broken)* is a *breakthrough*. The Lord is near to those who are experiencing a breakthrough in their hearts. A broken heart is often an opportunity for positive change when one's heart embraces the increase, multiplication, and prosperity a new breakthrough offers.

David was a man who constantly pursued after the heart of God; but do we understand the heart of David? We tend to be one dimensional believing our hurt is so severe that our broken heart is inconsolable. David used every negative, painful situation in life as an opportunity to get to know God in another dimension.

When one relationship or season ends, it is important to allow a period of time to elapse for healing and fine-tuning, while reflecting on both the good aspects and memories which remain and the bad attributes that should to be left behind and forgotten. It is important to make the needed adjustments before entering into a new relationship or alignment. This prevents one from carrying the negative personal issues into the new by rebounding or being attracted to the same hurtful elements or type of people again. God wants to take the forefront in our lives. He wants to be our number one love and obsession. He wants to wrap His loving arms around us to bring healing insights.

God will show us why the relationship did not work. During this transition time, our hearts are very tender, so it is important to renew our minds with God's Word after heartbreak. Fill the gaping emptiness with God's presence and not another relationship or you will end up repeating the same mistake.

David knew when his heart was broken it was from pursuing false gods or failing relationships. David had a heart that sought to understand God's heart. David turned to God as his suitor and the lover of his soul. God was waiting at the door to recapture David's heart. David constantly sought to be united with the heart of God. David knew his *broken heart* was an opportunity to surrender to the hand of God. Wounded hearts are very tender to God's presence. It requires a gentle touch while a wound is healing. This is why C.S. Lewis says, *"God whispers to us in our pleasures, speaks in our conscience, but shouts in our pains: it is His megaphone to rouse a deaf world."* God uses a megaphone during our pain. The pain we suffer requires a gentle touch while a wound is healing and every suggestion is loud on our tender wounded nerves. The wounds and hurts David endured, gave him an opportunity to experience the merciful touch of God's comfort in a fresh way.

What do you do when your heart is broken? Do you weep, mourn, detach, get angry, become depressed, or rebel? We express sorrow in many different ways. When we suffer a broken heart we want to be alone, so we isolate ourselves while we try to figure out what happened. These are normal responses and grieving must be allowed for a sufficient time. But, we should not allow painful wounds and sorrow to blind us to the Divine Suitor who is patiently waiting at the door of our heart to comfort us. We are never alone or abandoned God is always with us! God is ready to seize the opportunity to touch our heart. He is offering an opportunity, for breakthrough. Open your heart to God and feel His tender hand and His sweet breath upon you in a way you could have never felt when your life was full of joy, blessings and pleasures.

Heart Issues

In dreams our heart can represent romantic love because it is the center of affection and emotions. The heart can also represent pity or sympathy. The dreamer could be being warned to guard or watch over their heart, for out of it flow the wellspring or issues of life, *Proverbs 4:23*. The heart is the center of one's being and sensibilities, their mood, concern or sympathy, compassion, and affection. The heart appears in dreams to tell the dreamer to take courage, be strong, exercise their fortitude, loving devotion, and deepest feelings toward their loved ones.

God will give you the desires of your heart when you seek Him with all your heart. God will allow wisdom to enter your heart when you apply your heart to discipline and keep His commandments. We are not to envy others but keep our hearts clean by removing grief, anger, and arrogance that will deceive. Love God with all your heart, for where your heart is there your treasure is. Learn to forgive from the heart, so your heart will remain sensitive and feeling. If your heart appears hard or small in the dream, you may have the Grinch heart syndrome. Ask the Lord to heal your heart and grant you His love. When the love of God fills your heart it will expand. The more we love the more we live in abundance. The love of God brings hope; it is the greatest power and reality in the universe.

Don't Lose Your Head!

If you lose your head in dreams it may indicate you are not thinking clearly or you are not processing your situation in a logical manner. The loss of one's head can indicate one has lost their ability to reason correctly or that they are no longer following the teachings or protocol of Jesus who is the head of His body. The head can also represent God or the Lord. The head in dreams often represents who the person is, their identity, personality, intellect, attitudes and viewpoints on life.

The head represents the thoughts of the mind, one's opinions, one's mental power, decisions, intentions, self-image, authority, a husband, a father, a master, their boss, or the one in charge, such as the administrator, or CEO of a company.

If the head is being anointed with oil, it signifies one is called out or set apart for godly service. If there are hands holding a head it can represent grief, regret, or sorrow. To see someone else's head means you will meet or connect with a person of influence or status. But, to see your head severed it is a warning to use your head, not to lose your head through anger, worry or fear. You need to be led by the Spirit and not the intellect.

If there are two or more heads on one body then the person is being double minded, wavering, unstable in their ways, which leads to confusion. They are acting like a monster. However, if you notice that you are hosting several different heads, of those you respect or revere for their wisdom, the dream could indicate that two heads are better than one when it comes to solving difficult problems. You may need to get together with some trusted advisors, do some brainstorming and put your heads together.

If you see yourself washing lather from your head you will be sought out for your wisdom, counsel, and discernment. If you are scratching the head this signifies you are confused, perplexed or indecisive. But if your head is swollen or injured beware of pride, getting the "big head" or becoming full of arrogance, worry, doubt, fear, anxiety, mental frustration or a general lack of knowledge. The dreamer may have an unusually high opinion of oneself or be conceited. But a swollen head can also represent a possible medical condition or trauma involving the brain, such as a concussion.

Brain Pain

Along these same lines is the occurrence of dreams dealing with the brain or the lack of one's brain being present. Our brain is the command center of our body. It is the computer that receives input and stimulates the body to respond in the appropriate manner. Our brain houses our happy triumphs and fond memories as well as the traumatic incidences that leave us defeated or wounded. Things that affect our brain usually deal with a pattern of thinking we have developed or a certain misguided perspective that is causing us to make poor decisions.

Highly educated, brilliant people often dream of losing control of their brain. They have reported seeing an infestation of insects crawling in their ears to devour their brain as a delicious morsel. People who solve problems through intellectual ascent, thought, contemplation, and reasoning feel trapped or limited in jobs or relationships where they are not able to fully engage all their abilities. Their boss, who is represented by an alien, comes to zap their brain with a freeze ray gun every time he rejects their out-of-the-box ideas for a more traditional, safe approach. The dreamer may see their brain short-circuiting out, with sparks flying in all directions.

Others dream of inanimate objects or projectiles having to be surgically removed before creativity or new ideas are able to flow again. Seeing a brain in one's dream sends a message of think before acting, guard one's thoughts, and use thoughtfulness to reflect on your love for others. The brain represents intelligence, insights, and creativity. It is important to remember the lessons of the past, but there is also a need to learn new skills to insure a successful future. It is vitally important to renew the spirit of your mind with the Word of God, to tear down negative strongholds and thought patterns, while embracing good news.

Hair Brain

Hair and the condition of one's hair can tell us a lot about that person's self-image, their wisdom, understanding, authority and their thoughts. If they are sporting a new hairstyle, there have been some positive changes in one's attitudes or they have recently changed their mind on a certain issue. But conversely the dreamer may be trying to imitate someone they admire or they are jealous of by taking on their image or style. Often jealous women, who have divorced their husbands, will begin to model themselves after the beautiful woman who receives the attention or love from their ex-spouse. If she is not careful, she will lose herself by subconsciously or literally taking on the other woman's image. For example, if she is a brunette with brown eyes who discovers her ex-husband is dating a blonde with blue eyes, she may seek professional cosmetic help to transform herself into the blonde bombshell. If you have to change yourself, so as to appear like someone else, in order to compete or to gain a man's attention, you will never be able to successfully maintain that relationship. Eventually your roots will grow out and you will have to remove the blue contacts. If you can't be loved and accepted for who you are, then they are not the right person for you, move on, look somewhere else. You will always be the second best if you try to imitate someone else. But, if you embrace who you are in God, you will always be the best and only you!

If their hair is growing longer, they are gaining needed insights and wisdom to solve problems. But, on the other hand, long, lustrous hair can represent sensuality, sexual attraction, or seduction.

If they have pulled their hair back into a tight ponytail, they could be practicing some self-discipline, feeling restrained or limited or they may be returning to a simpler childlike time of dealing with things.

If one is wearing a wig when you don't own one, it could be a warning to the dreamer not to 'wig out' over negative thoughts, falsehoods, or bad attitudes.

Wildly tangled or unkempt hair can represent the person has a 'wild hair-brained' idea. The dreamer may be allowing their thought life to become unorganized, self-condemning, or hypercritical. They need to take some personal time to comb out these matted knots and smooth some matters out in their relationships.

Devoured by a Wild Beast

Another common dream sequence for people who are going through a divorce or separation is for some wild animal like a tiger to overcome them in a jungle setting, where it savagely devours their guts. Where great loss, gut wrenching pain, separation and even death of a loved one occurs, dreamers will experience their arms or legs being torn or severed from their torso. This severing of a relationship or tie leaves them feeling maimed, crippled, or helplessly devastated, unable to reach out or move forward. But through healing prayer and forgiveness their pain will subside. They will experience restoration and gain the needed strength to start life over again with someone new.

Receiving New Body Parts

When someone is losing a relationship or a life partner in a painful situation, their dreams will reflect a loss of body parts. The opposite is also true. When a new covenant relationship is born or a business partnership is formed, we tend to receive an additional limb or body part. We become like the bionic man or woman who is able to run faster and better than ever before. We become like Superman, able to leap over tall buildings in a single bound. We can see through brick walls with our laser vision. There aren't any obstacles we are not able to overcome with our new found strength, excitement and joy. Most dreams are symbolic, meaning that a certain symbol represents something else, but is not literal. But in some cases, the dreamer may be waiting for an organ transplant or be in need of a new body part in real life.

One example of this type of dream came through a little sixteen-year-old girl I will call Katie. Katie had kidney cancer. She was on a long waiting list of people who needed a new kidney. She had waited months for a call to be airlifted to receive a kidney transplant. The call finally came at a time when the family was not able to afford the plane ticket because they were in massive debt. The call came and the plane went but Katie was not on board. She was depressed knowing there would not be a second chance short of a miracle.

Katie and her mother came to a Renaissance fair in Whitehouse, Texas. That weekend the character theme at the fair was pirates and wenches. So Steven, my brother and I along with several other good dream interpreting friends, dressed up in full costume with eye patches and all.

We set up a dream interpretation booth under a beautiful oak tree at the entrance of the fair. Katie visited our booth. Katie's dream was simple but profound. She dreamed her cancer ridden kidney sprouted wings. It flew away in a golden windstorm, caught fire, and then returned to her healthy and vibrant.

When I met Katie she was despondent and depressed. Her mother was trying to distract her attention from her deadly situation by attending the fair. I asked Katie's mother to tell me her story. At first glance I thought Katie was an abuse victim. There were scars that looked like cigarette burns up and down her bare arms. But I was told those were from IV lines that had sustained her during previous organ transplant surgeries. Katie had already received a liver and a heart transplant. Her poor health had stunted her growth. She was very short in stature. She appeared as a ten year old who was sporting jet black-purple Kool-aide dyed hair that framed her snow-white skin and facial features. Unless God did a miracle under this oak tree, Katie didn't have long to live and she knew it.

Holy Spirit is the giver of life and gifts. That day He had a pair of new kidneys waiting for Katie. I asked her mother if I could pray for Katie. She said, "Sure, knock yourself out!" "All the great television evangelists and healers have prayed for her, but she has never felt anything before." I assured the mother I was not great but that I knew the Great One, Jesus!

As Katie took a seat in front of me the Holy Spirit began to show me His plan and strategy. He told me to ask, "Katie, do you realize there is not a breeze blowing, the wind is still and quiet?" Katie nodded her head yes. "The Holy Spirit is going to come as a gentle breeze in the top of this oak tree. When Holy Spirit brings His healing power the leaves will begin to rustle. This will be a sign to you that the cancer in your kidneys will be burned up by the Holy Spirit. God will do a Holy Spirit radiation treatment. Katie, when I lay my hands on you, you will feel warmth or a sensation like a cleansing fire moving in your lower back. Are you ready to receive your kidney transplant?" Katie nodded her head and closed her blue eyes. Moments later a gentle wind began to blow in the top of the majestic oak. I reached my hands around Katie to lay them on her cancerous kidneys. God's light literally shone from her face. Her once dark, depressed countenance was now sunny and bright. Her eye lashes began to flutter like butterfly wings. A tender stream of tears flowed down her now rosy red cheeks. I said, "You feel God don't you?" Katie sweetly shook her head, "Yes!" The Holy Spirit had come in His loving presence. As a wind, He blew over her from the top of the trees. His cleansing fire came to burn the cancer out of her kidneys. He brought a pair of healthy kidneys to Katie that day. What an amazing God we serve. Katie's dream came true.

Helping or Hurtful Hands

Hands represent power in our lives. Hands are used to reach out to others to draw them near or to push them away. Hands signify one's gifting or ability to obtain a future and a hope. Hands enable us to reach our destiny if they embrace and hold onto the right choices and people in life. Hands can both create and destroy. Hands represent our ability to develop relationships, helping friendships, self-expression and support of our children, family members and others. Hands grasp opportunities to serve or to show kindness as an extension of our power to give.

Waving goodbye represents a departure. Dirty, rough or unpleasant hands in the dream are a warning being issued to guard against wrong actions. While beautiful, clean, attractive, soft, well-groomed hands represent success and satisfaction in life. Busy or skilled hands represent prosperity, discipline, and achievement. Hands that are caressing others show love, affection, tenderness, and care. Bloody hands inspire thoughts of quarrels, feuds and murder. If one is washing their hands they are in the process of rectifying an injustice, hearing someone's case, or ridding yourself of any association, as Pilate did after his wife warned him not to have anything to do with convicting Jesus because He was innocent. If your hands are bound or tied, one is being bound to your word or agreement. There could also be a hindrance or limitation being imposed. This lets the dreamer know there are changes that are needed.

If the hand is bandaged or broken, it represents there will be momentary delays. It is also important to be aware of possible theft; it is time to review your accounting books. Hairy hands signify masculine strength, support or relationships bringing success. Shaking hands implies one is coming into agreement, a pledge or contract, by the giving of one's word; greeting a new friend, or a new introduction.

The right hand represents pleasures for ever more, faith, righteousness, fellowship with family or friends, a lover's embrace, a blessing, and wisdom to live a long life, Proverbs 3:16. The right hand also represents valiant skills bring the power to overcome and the strength to subdue, one's enemies; and the mark of the beast.

The left hand represents the wisdom to gain riches and honor. A lover's embrace with the left hand under a woman's head brings emotional security and healing in the Song of Solomon 2:6. The left hand also means that one is not satisfied; you need to give to the poor, be aware of trifling irritations and minor difficulties.

If a woman's hands are cut off, she needs to develop marketable skills so she can learn to take better care of herself instead of being totally reliant on her husband or family. Hands represent our skill levels, our capacity for positive or negative behaviors that we implement when we are in need. Hands help us make choices to grasp a bright future or remain trapped in our present dilemma.

The Face

The face is the part of our being that is seen the most by others. We always attempt to put our best face forward when we meet others or want to make a good impression. But, the face can also represent the false or a mask that is being worn to hide behind when we don't want to be truthful or reveal our true self. Who is that man in the mirror? The face represents a person's identity or image, their distinctive characteristics and facial features of how they are known and recognized.

Our face demonstrates the heart reflections or visage when we notice the expressions or facial features. The countenance will convey a message through its outward appearance. The face will exhibit their disposition, feelings or mood. If the face is disfigured in some manner or a foreign growth appears, the dreamer is being warned of an embarrassing situation that may represent some challenges. When the face is full of smiles there is happiness, success and joy in life. When God appears in our visions it is usually about a face to face encounter with intimacy. An all knowing, loving God has come to reveal Himself to us. When we come face to face with someone or something in our dreams it can represent intimacy with a friend, fading or increasing glory or a confrontation with an enemy.

When light meets any type of darkness, there is a confrontation. God's angels of light appear to battle dark, evil or demonic angels, but we are not able to recall their facial features. When angels or the Holy Spirit appear in our dreams we often refer to them as faceless people or friends who came to lead or guide us out of a bad situation. If our face is sad, we may be walking through difficulties, failure, sorrow or grief. We are to face, encounter or confront both difficult and desirable situations. This may cause us to change directions or take an about-face strategy in life. The earth also has a face. To dream of a face could indicate something on a very large scale taking place on the face of the earth.

The Liver

Every dream and each dream symbol has something to offer the dreamer. Ask yourself why was the liver chosen to be displayed in my dream? Why was that particular body organ chosen to communicate a message? Sometimes there is a play on words for example liver- "lover", "He makes my liver quiver," or better yet "liver" the person who lives life to the fullest. When living life becomes a challenge because of all the demands and varied directions our time and attentions are drawn to; the liver may appear in our dreams to remind us to live a little.

The liver is the organ that is responsible for filtering out poisons or toxins that are introduced to our digestive system. Because of its function, it may also represent irritability or that an inner cleansing is needed. Our liver also filters alcohol from our blood system so a possible change in diet is needed in connection to one's alcohol consumption. The dreamer may also find themselves having to process a toxic situation or feelings of fault finding or deceit.

The Mouth

No one wants to be known as a 'big mouth.' If our mouth is known for speaking words of wisdom and counsel then people will cherish the sweet words we speak. The mouth can be known for many different things. It can speak as a witness or testify, experience romantic, sensual pleasures in a kiss and a mouth can bite off more than it can chew.

Pay close attention to the mouth's condition. Is it a mouth of gossip when it is open? Or is it able to receive physical nourishment; or produce spiritual prayers chewing on the loving words of wisdom or speaking forth godly advice and grace. Since we only have one mouth it is important that we develop our listening skills twice as much and learn to talk less. We will give an account for every idle or hurtful word we speak, so let's keep short accounts. By our own words we will be justified or condemned.

The Nose Knows

Everyone remembers the Kellogg's Fruit Loops commercial with the Toucan who says, "Follow Your Nose, the Nose Always Knows!" But, this is also a true statement for dreamers. The nose is often the symbol of discerning good or evil intent. Then sadly, there are those who are always sticking their big nose in other people's business, the nosey snoop who is smitten with curiosity or the obnoxious community gossip who likes to sniff out controversy and spread harmful rumors.

If one's nose is bleeding in the dream there may be some facts that are getting twisted. This causes undue strife, which indicates the need to hone spiritual discernment, or pay attention to one's intuition. A nosebleed can also indicate financial loss or ruin is coming if changes are not made to stop a negative flow. If someone is blowing their nose in a dream it can indicate a decrease of unwanted obligations. You are getting rid of things that have buggered up your time. If you continue seeing your nose, it portends of friends and popularity, but a snub nose of pride warns against gossip, arrogance or conceit. If you are having difficulty breathing, because of a clogged nose, beware of hindrances or hidden obstacles.

Muscles

Strong muscles mean the dreamer has been dedicated to working things out to insure success and fitness. He is no stranger to using physical exertion and strength to make his way straight. He is operating on a natural level, where physical movement is needed and can be demonstrated by exhorting one's power and authority in certain areas of expertise. If someone's muscles appear weak, then failure and hardships will not be overcome when a hired thug or someone tries to strong-arm a frail individual. Trust in God and the power of prayer to bind and overcome the strongman. If the muscles appear sore or painful, someone is in emotional or physical distress. When someone displays their muscles or strength, it could represent that they are going through a time of frustration or intimidation. By flexing their muscles they are attempting to encourage themselves or cause a threat to back off the opposition.

Paralysis

In dreams where the body is paralyzed, it signifies a demonic entity that brings the presence of fear. At times when angels appear a person is also paralyzed. Paralysis can also indicate that the dreamer is afraid to make decisions; they may be in an emotionally traumatic experience; wrestling with a spiritual presence or they are battling with their own conscience. Ask God for His wisdom and strategy of faith which counters fear. Even a small measure of faith will overcome fear and bring freedom.

Pregnancy

Contrary to popular belief, both men and women can become pregnant in dreamland. Pregnancy indicates that you are expanding. There are new areas of one's life potential or personality that are developing. One is being prepared for something new. It is on the way, but this new venture will require a time of preparation and development before it arrives. After this new thing manifests, it will require a lot of attention and skill in nurturing. Material wealth and happiness is growing. God's prophetic promises are being birthed. They will be fulfilled through the process of reproduction. Labor pains indicate you have entered into the final test, trial, or push before the new venture, relationship or ministry is delivered into your hands. When a man is pregnant in a dream it can also be a warning for him to guard against indiscriminate sex or the way he treats women with disrespect or contempt.

Shoulder

The shoulders represent one's authority, power, and ability to support and govern by taking responsibility as the need arises, or to bear up under the changes in life and what those changes bring. If your shoulders are thin or weak you are depending too much on other's support or influence. If you see yourself massaging someone's shoulders while they are resting on you, it means you are giving them more authority or power to support you in life.

The Skin

The skin represents an outward protection of social and physical boundaries. The skin keeps us from too much contact with others or the world. The skin is the body's largest organ; it allows one to be in touch with or experience the world. The skin represents the feeling or senses one uses to interact with people. If one's skin is missing, you are feeling exposed, vulnerable, untouchable, and you need to construct some limits and safe boundaries in your life.

No one likes to be stripped of their dignity, skinned alive or taken advantage of. If the skin is smooth there will be happiness. If the skin is rough that person possesses a harsh exterior or personality. Blotchy skin means there will be troubled spots or embarrassments in relationships. Burnt skin foretells of hurt or that one will be devastated or burned in a relationship. If your skin is peeling, it is time to change one's ways. You are going through a metamorphous. When the process is completed, you will be more sensitive to your own needs and the desires of those around you. Or you are healing from being burned and true happiness is on the way.

The Spine

The spine is a specialized support structure that enables one to feel sense and move through life. If one has a strong backbone it indicates they have courage, an inner resolve or fortitude. They are able to make a bold stand, even if the odds or popular opinion is against them. On the other hand if they are spineless, they are lacking the needed courage or willpower to make a positive productive difference in life.

The Throat

Some ladies are selected as models because they possess a long beautiful, attractive throat. Their beauty opens doors for them to rise to prominence on the cover of fashion magazines. Necks or throats are often seen as elegant beauty. The neck connects our thought life, moral belief and opinions with our physical actions and chosen lifestyle. The throat represents a narrow passage that could make it possible to communicate openly, as represented with the use of a harsh or guttural voice. Sometimes the opinions of others are too large to swallow and if they force the issue, we may feel choked on their words. If the throat suffers harm or injury in some way the dreamer is vulnerable to control. If they experience strangulation with a rope the dreamer may hang himself with his own words or by repeating the negative words of others. They are in danger of losing their head. If hands are chocking your throat you may have submitted yourself to a wrong influence that is trying to remove the breath of life. A throat can also depict an open grave in *Psalm 5:9*, or Sheol, in *Isaiah 5:14*. If a knife is being held to one's throat in a dream, it means to use self-control or your excessive appetites need to be reined in *Proverbs 23:2*.

For a comprehensive list of thousands of body parts and their symbolic meanings in dreams please avail yourself to Dream Encounters Symbols Volumes I & III at www.BarbieBreathitt.com

Chapter 7
Buildings, Rooms & Structures

A skillful architect first imagines plans and then she carefully draws the design of a building or beautiful structure according to the exact measurements of the blueprint so the edifice will serve a specific purpose or function. The designer places a part of her fingerprint on each room, chamber, hallway and porch. Every square inch reflects her DNA yet resonates with its own distinct glory. The beauty of the exterior windows, doors, arches and the slope of the roof draw the admiring eyes and attention of those who pass by. The human body was fashioned by the Architect of the Universe out of the dust of the ground. God formed man in His image and likeness with His hands. Then God blew the breath of life into Adam so he became a living being. God's original plan, design and blueprint were to make His habitation with and in man. The Holy Spirit still dwells within the hearts of man not in houses made with human hands. Believers are the sacred temples of the Holy Spirit.

The dreams we dream give us insights into the person God has created us to be. The long hallways we travel during times of transition and decision making give us entrance into new doors that open to rooms we have never seen before. There we discover gifts, talents and abilities we have not tapped into yet. These chambers are parts of our life that have lain dormant until we discern them in the fullness of time. After a period of preparation we are now ready to step through the door. We cross the threshold into a fresh chapter in life to explore the breadth, length, height and depth of God's vast love dawning on the horizon.

Our dreams can depict us living in previous homes from our childhood or distant past. Or our dreams may feature us in some futuristic space station in the outer realms of space. Seeing your own house in a dream is one of the most common dream symbols. Houses represent you. They can also symbolize the unconscious center of our emotion or psychological self, which is not fully known by our mind. All of our conscious and subconscious familiarity, memories and developmental stages of life may be represented by various houses or rooms that appear in our dream. They are often full of intricate details that cause our minds to wonder why these facts have been included. When we discover each of their varied meanings we discover new and interesting aspects about our potential, giftings, talents and purpose of being alive.

The homes we find ourselves dwelling in usually do not resemble our present day homes. Often the houses we encounter in our dreams are nothing like the homes we have occupied in our waking life. We may keep returning to the same house, which never existed in our waking life. Visiting past dwelling places in our dreams enables us to explore our unconscious thoughts and fading memories. These houses have rooms and hidden chambers we have never seen before. The hallways of transition seem to stretch on into eternity and never come to an end.

The house we occupy is a representation of ourselves and our present mental condition. It reflects our perspectives on life and is a barometer that allows us to determine how we are feeling about our present circumstances or how they are affecting us. *Jesus said, "Do not let your heart be troubled; believe in God, believe also in Me." "In My Father's house are many dwelling places; if it were not so, I would have told you; for I go to prepare a place for you. If I go and prepare a place for you, I will come again and receive you to Myself, that where I am, there you may be also." John 14:1–4 NASU*

Jesus is the door that leads to the Father in heaven. Jesus is the carpenter and architect, who's building the New Jerusalem. We are the pillars, rooms, dwelling places, houses and mansions. *"And I saw the holy city, the New Jerusalem, coming down out of heaven from God. It was prepared like a bride dressed for her husband. I heard a loud voice from the throne. It said, "Now God's home is with people. He will live with them. They will be his people. God himself will be with them and will be their God. He will wipe away every tear from their eyes. There will be no more death, sadness, crying, or pain. All the old ways are gone." Revelation 21:2-4*

If we visit a familiar home in our dreams that was occupied in our waking life, think about the memories that are associated with it. A dream about being in a childhood home can indicate a need to face unanswered conflicts that were ignited in childhood. Or it can show a desire to return to a simpler time of childhood innocence when we were nurtured and taken care of by others in a safe, peaceful place.

To dream of visiting the home of someone you know, a friend or acquaintance may mean that you admire that person. Also you may be in need of, or desire the characteristics, nature, or the qualities that you attribute to that person. For example, to find yourself in the home of a big-hearted person, you may feel unloved, restricted or in need of others' openhandedness, or generosity. How are you behaving in life? Are you a giving or a stingy person? Do you forgive others? Are you hard on yourself? Being in the home of someone who is an exhorter may indicate you are being too critical.

The Attic

The attic is the place where we store our memories and artifacts. It allows us to see the frame of mind we are in and whether our thoughts are positive or negative. Since attics are at the top of a house it can represent a need of higher learning, a higher level of thinking godly thoughts or an elevation in problem solving skills. Attics are usually featured in scholarly people's dreams that enjoy research and intellectual pursuits.

If the attic is jammed full of old relics or antiques that are covered with sheets and layered with dust, it indicates the dreamer is in a season of confusion. They have developed some antiquated mental strongholds or old ways of thinking that are not compatible with their present situation. There is a need to renew the mind with the Word of God to gain higher wisdom and elevated spiritual insights.

The Basement

The basement often shows the character flaws or foundational issues in our lives that need to be corrected or strengthened. If the foundation has not been laid on good moral and godly principles the dreamer will often find cracks that allow water to come in to flood their basement. In real life our basements are usually full of stuff we collected over time. In our dreams, we may find some very unusual, fearful and surprising things in our basements. A dark basement is a great place to conceal our animalistic carnal natures. These are the primitive or unacceptable parts of us that we have tried to keep under wraps, but they keep hanging around like bats dangling from the ceiling. We have killed or attempted to murder their surplus influences. These unwanted personality traits will appear as dead bodies, snakes, or tigers or other wild animals that we have kept caged or hidden from our friends and family.

Basements are psychological filing cabinets where we store things we are not willing to let go. Things in our basement represent the negative resources or hurtful issues we are still painfully sorting through.

Basements can also show us areas in our bodies that are not functioning to their full capacity. Like a slow burning furnace that indicates our metabolism has slowed down and is not burning the calories it used to. An old rusty pump that is not working to full capacity can represent a clogged artery or heart that is not pumping the proper amount of blood; resulting in high or low blood pressure. A knotted mess of wires that look like a bowl of spaghetti can represent kinked clogged arteries that are in immediate need of attention. A tangled hose can represent intestinal problems. Metal plumbing or plastic pipes can represent a blocked circulatory or nervous system. Taking inventory of the tools we find in the basement can add years to our lives.

The Backyard

A dream that is set in the context of a backyard scene represents that one is keeping aspects of their past life secret or hidden from view. They have a lack of openness that will lead to emotional poverty and cause them to live their present life as if they are still living in the past. The backyard represents the ordinary terrain in our lives that the dreamer often takes for granted. Backyards speak of our past history of accomplishments or the potential that we already possess that when tapped into will cause a successful future without exerting much effort. If something negative keeps appearing in your backyard it is a warning to remove pessimistic attitudes or reactions that can zap your forward momentum. It is time to complete half done or old projects or business ideas that have been pushed aside so they do not continue to hold you back.

The Bathroom

The bathroom is a place where we undergo emotional, physical or spiritual cleansing. We go there to wash away negative, hurtful attitudes or dirty thoughts. A new look or refreshing comes through the process of renewing the spirit of your mind. Taking a shower symbolically represents the person is washing away hurt feelings, offenses and the stain of sin and mistakes. We are able to flush unwanted waste down the drain, letting forgiveness come to remove bitter issues. If the shower is interrupted by someone's presence being introduced during your shower they may have the needed words of wisdom to help remove things from the past especially if they are washing your back.

If there is a plumbing problem where the drains or the toilet is backing up or running over it indicates a flood of negative feelings or stinking thinking that is overwhelming the communication lines are clogged. You are having difficulty processing or expressing your feelings adequately. These emotional overloads may not be the way you would typically respond to any given situation but you are feeling weighted down or swamped at the moment. The dreamer needs to take a deep breath and reprioritize his or her life, making sure they include some valuable 'me time' in the mix. Stop being a dumping ground. Don't allow people to regurgitate or spew their poisonous in your hearing that is a waste of your valuable time. What good can come from them pouring their negative opinions, filth and squalor on you? Set firm boundaries and make a clean start.

Flush the Toilet

A dream that you need to have a bowel movement or urinate can be based on a real physical sensation or need to use the toilet. But, elimination dreams can also have an emotional cause. When we dream of relieving ourself of body waste it can represent the eradication of unhealthy, harmful thoughts and negative, toxic or depressing emotions. Feeling the need to urinate can also be caused by sexual stimulation. In the world of dreams the presence of water is often associated with the emotional realm. So urinating can deal with the need to flush negative, hurtful emotions, such as anger, hatred or jealousy. Seeing one's self defecating or straining because of constipation can indicate you have been stuffing your emotions or that we are carrying psychological baggage or emotional burdens you need to free yourselves from. Ask the Holy Spirit oil to lubricate your inner man. Allow forgiveness to take place so cleansing can come to start the flow or elimination of harmful thoughts removing poisonous toxins of sin and bondage.

Where's the Toilet?

A very common dream that people experience when they have repressed their thoughts or emotions is they are in desperate need to urinate or have a bowel movement, but they can't find a bathroom or a clean toilet. All the bathrooms are already in use, have no privacy door, or they are unavailable. The toilets that you find are filthy, over-flowing or out of order. The disgusting stench is nauseating. The mucky toilet paper over flows and the floor you're standing on is covered with brown waste.

Dreaming that you have to use the bathroom in front of others may indicate that you fear others uncovering your deepest, darkest secrets or you don't know how to express yourself adequately. If others are watching you use the toilet then it also indicates they will see you getting free of the wasteful things that have filled you up, hindered or weighed you down. They will see you flush the past, wash your hands of them and make a stand by taking your first steps towards a new fresh start.

Showering or Bathing

Taking a bath or shower in a dream often represents the process of cleansing yourself mentally, physically, emotionally or spiritually. It is time to transform yourself by renewing your mind and enhancing your physical state of being. Get rid of mental strongholds, negative or critical thought processes and bad habits.

Coiffuring

We all want to look our best and put our best face forward. First impressions are often lasting impressions. When we dream of grooming ourselves in a bathroom, it can represent an effort to conceal from others the characteristics of ourselves that we don't like.

To dream of seeing yourself gazing into a bathroom mirror indicates you are going through a transformation process, change or metamorphosis. You are being transformed from one realm of existence into a higher, better state of existence. It is time to take a look at your real self and come clean. You are being given an understanding of who you have been created to become. It is time to let go of the hidden things that have entrapped the old man of the past and become the innovative person with a new identity. See yourself in a new light and embrace the needed changes to remake your image.

Dreams of washing, combing or brushing hair indicates wisdom is being given to straighten out situations concerning your covering. This wisdom will bring strength into your waking situations so you can untangle snares or negative entrapments in situations. This new strength and wisdom will enable you to maintain control where boundaries have been violated.

Razor Sharp

Shaving your legs in a dream can symbolize a desire to change your walk in life. Shaving your arm pits indicates you will be ridding yourself of a negative relationship that has caused a lot of embarrassment by making a real stink in your life. To shave your face means you are ready to make some changes that will enhance the way people perceive you. You will have a clean cut image as you enter into this next positive phase of life. To shave the hair on your head may indicate that you are not making good use of wisdom that would cover you from making a bad mistake in judgment.

It's Time to Make-up not Cover-up

We all want to be accepted for who we are, but at times we hide our true feelings or desires, which is a form of deception. If you are applying cosmetics in a dream, you may be trying to cover up your true self in order to fit in with a certain crowd or conform to the expectations of a particular person. Applying makeup may also indicate you have a need to humble yourself before others, ask for forgiveness and 'makeup' with those you have wronged or offended. Then applying makeup can also indicate you are making yourself appear better or enhancing your positive attributes since, as the expression goes, "every old barn can use a new coat of paint."

The Bedroom

I love to spend a lot of quiet time in the privacy of my bedroom. It is a quiet place where I can escape from social demands and rest. I enjoy taking a nap, praying or taking time to read the Bible or a good book on the sofa. When I was a child, mom and dad retired to the bedroom to have adult conversations. I knew better than to disturb them. The bedroom is a place of intimacy, where a husband and wife make love and hold each other close in a warm embrace. The bedroom is also a symbolic place that represents sexuality, reproduction and increase. Bedroom scenes in dreams can let us know when there are other things, like a demanding boss, career ambitions or nosey relatives that are coming between your sexual or intimate family times. These dream characters will often appear or barge into the bedroom when they have been given too much influence in your waking lives.

Buildings

The buildings in our dreams represent one's self-image or the body. There are often different floors or layers that have significant meanings. The dreamer is making positive progress; awareness and understanding is being made if one is on upper levels; while the lower levels reflect foundational or primitive attitudes. Before we take on a building project or some new venture in our lives, it is important to count the cost before beginning. If we are prepared and have the needed resources, the shiny new building with green lawns will represent prosperity, plenty, and success. But if the building appears old and things are decaying we may need to put things on hold and reevaluate our position.

In our dreams a new building represents a happy, profitable life, while if the building is ruined or damaged one should immediately change one's approach to a relationship or job situation. If the building is collapsing their self-image has suffered a blow; their pursuit of material gain is failing. They are losing sight of their goals or ambition. If someone is falling off a building, they are failing in a task or unconsciously descending instead of being successful in their pursuits. If the dreamer is scaling or climbing the outside of a building it indicates their ambitious drive will cause their success by leaps and bounds.

Foundational Issues

Every architect, building contractor or structural engineer knows that in order to build a sturdy building one must have a solid, firm foundation. If the foundation of the structure is not big or strong enough, the building will not be properly aligned or squarely supported. If the foundation is cracked, eventually the walls will crack. Jesus said He would show us what our lives would be like if we only listened to the Words of His teaching but did not build them into our waking lives. *Luke 6:48–49 says, "It is like a person building a house, who digs deep and lays the foundation on solid rock. When the floodwaters rise and break against the house, it stands firm because it is well-built. But anyone who hears and doesn't obey is like a person who builds a house without a foundation. When the floods sweep down against that house, it will collapse into a heap of ruins." NLT*

Often dreams of a house, room, building and other structures can give us needed clues to help us build a successful life for ourselves, our friends and loved ones. The amazing thing about dreams is that in a dream anything is possible. Dreams are not limited by any physical laws, such as gravity or finances. When the dreamer surveys the blueprints or architectural plans for their new house, they may be surprised that the toilet is located in the kitchen or living room for that matter. Thankfully these details don't reflect our real homes in real time. No one would want to entertain guests at a dinner party with a porcelain throne perched next to the kitchen's island carving block.

Corridor

A long corridor or passageway indicates that one is exploring some new dimensions of himself by moving from one place to another in a transitional period of life. During this process of spiritual enlightenment and emotional transformation, one's physical dexterity and proficiency will provide an open passageway or access doors to new ways of thinking. Compulsive, harmful behavior patterns need to be broken to begin a new upward cycle.

Doors

Doors represent opportunities if they are open or an invitation to come up higher to explore potential changes. If something is blocking the door don't give up; keep knocking until you get the desired answers. However, it is also possible that God is jamming this door to avail you to a bigger and better opening in the future. If someone is knocking on a front door it means that an opportunity is presenting itself now or in the near future. Doors represent both positive and negative choices or directions that are being offered. Doors give unexpected entrances to a new experience so we can leave the old behind during times of transition. Doors make it possible for us to step forward into the new. When unwanted changes are forcing themselves upon us, we often dream of a scary, large intruder trying to force his way through the door into our safe home.

Do not sit idly by to wait for opportunity to knock at your door; create it. Your now and future prosperity depends upon your ability to imagine yourself rising above obstacles and accomplishing your purposed destiny. The dreams you hold within your heart are revealed through the words you express in prayer. Jesus is the only door that gives us access to God the Father. Prayer leads to an intimate relationship. It is not a technique, program or formula to get what you want from God.

When you pray find a quiet, secluded place; be as simple and honest as possible. Do not change who you are or the way you communicate to put on some theatrical act before God. Shift your focus from yourself onto the love and grace God offers. When you sense the lingering presence of the Holy Spirit manifesting, listen for His still small voice and follow His lead. When the Holy Spirit is done speaking, pray what is on your heart in response to what He has shared. Prayer is an art of two way communication between God and man. Words are more powerful than most people realize. The dreams you dream, the thoughts you think and the words you express form your world. Everyone has access to creativity. What kind of world will your prayer life and imagination create for you?

Women will dream of a tall, dark stranger coming to their door to romance them when a desire to develop or they have already met a new love interest. When a new relationship is dawning the themes of a woman's dreams will alert her to some unconscious feelings. If she is fearful of rejection or of sharing her true self, she may dream of being burglarized, raped or invaded by a shadowy figure. She may begin to dream of a masked man that could be her own psyche attempting to sabotage the relationship before it has time to grow. If her spirit is whole and ready for a new door to open in her life she will gladly embrace and explore the possibilities with this new Romeo.

Doors allow us to gain entrance into new opportunities, but if they are locked they can also keep us from stepping into our future or destiny. We may feel like someone or something is trying to keep us locked out or shut down through imposing strict limitations on our gifts and talents. A time of prayer and spiritual reflection will show you where the keys are that will unlock this door of destiny. Is there a weakness, character flaw or an addiction to work, an individual or substance that is keeping you from being the successful person you are meant to be? Once you discover the keys that unlock your success, be willing to make the necessary changes and the doors will spring open. If you see someone leaving through the back door exit in a dream, this can indicate they will be passing away or leaving your life.

Front Yard or Porch

The front yard or a front porch indicates that a current or future vision is being given. Where as a backyard or back porch indicate past memories or events that have already transpired. If you are in the process of building a front porch in your dream a new level of increase is coming to brighten your future. Front porches represent a place where you relax in a rocking chair to share your hopes and dreams of a bright future with close friends and family while sipping on a cold iced tea.

The Home

The state of the residence indicates one's current physical, emotional or spiritual condition. If the home is dilapidated it can indicate the dreamer is tired, worn out, full of sorrow, sickness or in need of healing, repair and rest. A home in this poor condition lets the dreamer know that their failure is insured unless they remedy these physical conditions.

In contrast, if the dreamer is going to a cheery home it indicates that their family brings them a lot of pleasure, joy and fulfillment. They find comfort and harmony when they are with the ones who share their home. If the home is being remodeled it is important for the dreamer to evaluate where they are in life. They take steps to tear out their old, outdated appliances or applications, make positive productive changes and update their thinking, so that they can be more successful and move forward.

The Kitchen

The kitchen reveals the heart motives of a matter, "If you can't take the heat stay out of the kitchen." The kitchen is the place where a loving man or woman, creative friend, nurturing mother or wife prepares food for her husband, guest and children. We often think of the cliché, 'we are what we eat' in conjunction with kitchens. Spiritual, emotional and physical food is prepared in a kitchen setting. The chef is often able to take an array of leftovers and like magic they can create a most delicious meal with very little effort.

Life doesn't always give us a bowl of cherries. Sometimes that bowl is full of pits and someone else has enjoyed the fruits of our labors. When we are left with the pits, it is our attitude that will determine if we will be successful or fail by falling into a victim's mentality. When life gives us a bowl of cherry pits, dig a hole and bury them. Water and cultivate that garden and before too long those dry pits will turn into a cherry orchard. When you harvest the cherries you can make cherry pies for all your friends who offered you support in your time of need.

The kitchen is a place that allows us to make something beautiful out of the sometimes-negative aspects of life. I'm not one to follow the directions in a cookbook. I had much rather experiment on my own. A kitchen allows you to tap into your strengths and try new things in a safe environment. Notice the equipment that is available to you. Is the kitchen clean, spacious, modern and inviting, or cluttered, outdated, infested and dirty? If you have taken on too many projects with too little time to complete them, your sink will be full of dirty pots and pans. Of if you are spreading yourself too thin and you don't have time to give the proper amount of attention to your significant other, it is time to take them off the back burner; move them to the forefront again. A kitchen should project a sunny, happy place where grandmother used to bake your favorite cookies or her award winning carrot cake.

The Living Room

In dreams the living room often speaks of our memories of everyday life in general terms. It shows us a place of fellowship or communion where we spend time with our family and friends. If our employer and work associates continue to occupy a prominent place in our living room this can indicate we need to leave our work in the office and stop bringing it home with us. To have a healthy life we need times of rest, play, and leisure to pursue personal interests, hobbies and vacation. Everything needs to be in proper balance and rhythm. If the living room appears to be over crowded or includes furniture from other areas of the home, church or office this is a good indication the dreamer has allowed people to violate safe healthy boundaries. It is time to put everything in your life back into proper order.

The Hallway

A hallway represents a transition or journey into the unknown. There is some level of self-exploration and the beginning of a new life path. The dreamer may explore spiritual enlightenment, emotional healing, physical or mental passage into new opportunities. A hallway can represent a time in one's life where there are not a lot of options readily available. The narrow hallway keeps the dreamer moving forward from one area to a new place in time. Doors may appear along the hallway. When multiple doors appear, ask for wisdom to choose the correct door of access. Then begin to knock on doors to see which ones will open. Unlock one door at a time to see what opportunities are awaiting you?

Passageway

A long hall or passageway represents new opportunities, relationships or an exhilarating occurrence that stimulates a new outlook or attitude toward life. During the dream the dreamer may decide to do some partial exploration instead of opening all the doors that appear in the passageway. It is important to seek godly wisdom and advice to receive full knowledge of options that these doors are offering, to be able to benefit to the fullest extent.

Past Homes or Dwellings

As we journey through our life we will find ourselves in assorted and varied hotels, apartments, trailers, houses, condos, patio homes and dormitories. Each of these temporary or permanent homes holds significance. Take note of the environment that appears as each home is viewed in your dream. What types of memories come to the surface? How did that house make you feel? Were they happy or sad times? Were you important or insignificant? What are some positive steps you can take to ease your present situation?

It is a common occurrence to dream about the homes where we lived in the past. It does not mean we are stuck in some kind of a time warp or we never moved on in life. Each home we occupied represents a certain period of time in our life. Some of those times were carefree, safe times with loving parents or grandparents who took care of us. But, for others who were not fortunate enough to have loving, supportive or protective parents or guardians that home represents a time of fear, neglect, abuse and uncertainty.

Our first dwelling becomes the dream symbol that represents our family home to us. We still remember and often practice the same holiday traditions we learned as a child. The homes in our dreams reveal the way we are feeling about our current living conditions and the resources we need to help us get through those times. Look at your current life setting and what is happening in your life. Ask yourself why you would need to or even want to go back to that particular childhood home. Recall any good or bad habits, any social patterns or ideas you may have obtained there and then make the necessary adjustments.

Windows

In dreams a window represents the dreamer's vision, their life views, perspectives or spiritual insights. If the window is open you are seeing an opportunity; one's potential or future hopes. God will open up the windows of heaven and pour out a blessing you will not be able to contain. But, in contrast, if the window is closed it is not yet time for the things you are viewing to come to pass. If someone is sitting in a window, they are content just watching life passing by, so they need to take a chance or start actively living again. To see someone climbing in a window indicates that dishonesty will be exposed. To climb out a window in a dream means there will be a narrow escape from calamity. If there is a window in the sky it represents an open heaven where great favor and increased blessing will begin to rain down on the dreamer.

For a comprehensive list of thousands of Buildings Structures & Rooms Dream Symbols please avail yourself to Dream Encounter Symbols Volume III at www.BarbieBreathitt.com

DREAM INTERPRETER

Chapter 8
Frequent Dream Categories

Anger

Anger is a natural emotion. Everyone gets angry at times. Although everyone gets angry we are erroneously taught that nice people don't get angry. We learn to stuff our angry emotions, deny our hurt feelings, and contradict it until anger becomes rage or depression. *"Be angry, but do not sin; do not let the sun go down on your anger" Ephesians 4:26–27*. If we do not resolve anger issues quickly they will give the devil an opportunity to bring negative influences into play. Once our anger begins to boil we can blow our tops. Our dreams will reflect the fact that we have lost our cool. Because we did not learn to express our anger in a healthy way when it first began, we will see ourselves explode in our dreams in an inappropriate manner. We may curse like a sailor, scream, and yell obscene words at the top of our lungs at friends, loved ones or our boss. We may pull someone's hair, slap their face, choke their neck or shoot them with a gun. We may run them down with our car, throw them off a cliff or drown them in a bathtub. We may ignite them with fire, nail them to a cross or leave them swinging from the end of a rope. All of these nightmarish dreams indicate we have let our anger build up until we are expressing it in an unhealthy manner.

When someone is expressing their anger towards you in an unhealthy manner it can indicate that you are a victim of their jealousy. Conversely, you may be feeling guilty for getting the credit for their good job being done at work or some great achievement or award they accomplished in life. Remember; do not limit yourself or your potential but always be honest and fair when dealing with others. We are all called to do great things in life.

Murder

To watch a spouse, friend or family member get harmed in a dream is a horrible, helpless feeling. No matter what the dreamer does they are not able to intervene or save their loved one from harm's way. The shock effects of this dream are devastating. No matter how loud you try to scream, no voice comes to the surface. Your arms and legs each weigh a ton and you're unable to run or reach out to stop the deadly blows from coming. The awful scene replays again and again and each time you are left with no strength. There is no possible way to help or protect your loved one from tragedy or death. These dreams are often due to the dreamer crowding their loved ones out of their life through over commitment, being a workaholic or staying too busy to relate. They listlessly watch as the most valuable things in their lives, their spouse or children, are stolen, abducted or murdered before their eyes.

Drowning

Mothers usually share a dream of the fear they feel of losing one of their children to drowning. They see a body floating face down in a dark pool of water. They rush to the water's edge to discover it is their dead son or daughter suspended in a watery grave. These dreams indicate there is a fear of losing their child through a lack of communication, love or parenting skills. Their fear of rejection or failure is very real; so the thing, which they fear, the most comes upon them.

Dreams of drowning can also indicate the dreamers is feeling overwhelmed or is overcome or flooded by negative emotions in their waking life. Maybe deadlines and unpredictable schedules at work are raining on them with a torrential downpour. Things are coming so quickly that you are not able to catch your breath. You feel like you are not able to continue treading water to keep your head above the surface. You know that each time you are able to pull yourself back up to the surface to gasp for another breath it may be your last. You are trying desperately to hold on, but you know if something doesn't change quickly you are going down for the last time.

Running Away or Chasing Dreams

What are you afraid of? What type of situations or emotional upheavals will cause you to retreat or run away? What type of negative or alarming situations are taking place in your waking life? Are you able to confront difficulties to resolve them or do you simply withdraw, run away or ignore conflict? Sometimes we are being chased by a lion in our dreams. A lion can represent Satan as a roaring lion walking the earth, seeking someone to devour. But a lion may also represent Jesus, the Lion of the Tribe of Judah, walking the earth seeking someone to bless. If you start running in your dreams, you will have to continue running for years until you are exhausted and finally have to stop, turn around and boldly face your fears. Dream characters will continue to advance and chase you as long as you run. Determine in your heart that God has not given you a spirit of fear but of love, courage and a sound mind. Never allow fear to prevail. Exercise your faith in an all-knowing, all-powerful God. If your trust lies in His loving arms you will be able to overcome any and everything that tries to chase you off the road of destiny.

Out of Control

When the dreamer's emotions are out of control, their dreams will often reflect those feelings. A frequent out of control dream theme is equipment that begins to malfunction or break down. The car, which often represents their life, will begin to accelerate to dangerous speeds on crowded highways or city streets. Although the brake pedal is mashed through the floorboard, the car continues to barrel through every roadblock, careening off into the oncoming traffic. No matter how bad the dreamer tries to stop or slow down, the vehicle races forward. This is a good time to discern the area in your life that is charging ahead of or crashing into your comfort zone. Have you started a new career, a relationship or have you taken on new responsibilities you are not prepared for? When the necessary adjustments are made, you will once again be able to gain adequate control over your vehicle and balance your life.

I Can't Find My Purse or Wallet

This is a frequent dream that is very troubling. The thoughts of fear come rushing in. Did someone steal my purse or wallet when I wasn't looking? Or have I momentarily lost my mind by leaving it unattended? Am I that irresponsible? Have I lost my keys, identity, my drivers' license, my money and all of my credit cards? Am I a victim of identity theft? Where is the last place I remember having my purse? Frantically, we begin to search and we panic. We retrace our steps trying to locate our missing purse or wallet. Each time we arrive at a previous location the wallet is not there. We are stranded with no money to pay our bill. We can't call for help because our phone is in the purse. We can't drive anywhere because our car keys are also missing. Feelings of hopelessness and despair come crashing in.

A lost purse or wallet dream produces a lot of fear and anxiety. The dreamer is usually experiencing a lot of confusing transitions or uncertain changes in their waking life. The loss of a purse or wallet may indicate that the dreamer is in the middle of a move to a new geographic region or embarking on a career change. They may feel like they are losing their identity due to getting old, the empty nest syndrome or retiring from a meaningful career. New seasons, relationships or possibilities are being introduced and they feel like they are losing touch with the familiar.

When these dreams begin to surface it is important to minimize the fear of uncertainty and get connected to a strong support system of friends. You may need to seek someone out who is a good listener so you can openly discuss your anxious feelings and worries. Find a trusted friend or counselor who can give you some needed stability, comfort or advice. Sometimes simply talking things out with a friend can remove the feelings of anxiety, abandonment or the uncomfortable feeling of being disoriented in some new surroundings.

Most people find comfort in connecting or reconnecting to God in a stronger way to gain His wisdom. By surrendering and placing their faith, trust and desires in God they are able to come to a place of rest. Knowing that God has a plan that will cause their success brings a needed peace Jeremiah 29:11. The sense of loss departs; and hope is restored when faith increases.

DREAM

Title: Purses

Wake time: 6:00 a.m. (*1 Kings 6:18–35*, speaks of open flowers in the temple Solomon built.)

I was going back to this building to get my belongings. I was collecting clothes and put on an apron. I could see these flowered pants that I had on underneath. I lost my purse but then I found it again. I also found all the other purses that I had lost. Women were bringing me the lost purses. I also saw a woman that had died on a table, covered with a plastic flowered tablecloth that had to be split in the middle, because it was too small to cover her whole body.

Interpretation

This dream indicates that you are returning to some past issues (going back to this building). Clothes speak of different coverings, mantels or different anointings. You are 'collecting' or remembering your hopes and past dreams. You are a diligent worker (apron). Even in your work, you saw the beauty (flowered pants) and favor of the Lord's fragrance underneath all your efforts.

A purse speaks of a person's identify, their self-worth. You have had many 'lost' purses. Have you had issues with a dampened identity? Or suffered from a poor self-image? Has someone spoken negative words over you or to you in the past? Are there any issues of abuse? In the dream, you 'found ' your true identity in Christ.

You may have a call to minister to or with other 'women' who have lost their self-worth (lost purses). The 'women' had experienced some type of spiritual or emotional death. Her life seems to have been split down the middle or divided or covered by a thin flimsy 'plastic flowered tablecloth,' empty, lifeless but 'flowered' on the outside so no one knows the pain!

This dream is showing you where you will be going. You will experience a healing and recovery (found the purse again) of your image. You will also assist others along your journey. This is a good dream of promise!

DREAM

Title: Lost and Found

Wake up time: 11:00 a.m. (*John 11:39, speaks of Lazarus as deceased) Jesus said, "Remove the stone." Martha, the sister of the deceased, said to Him, "Lord, by this time there will be a stench, for he has been dead four days."*)

Mike's name means esteemed; Who is like God? *Exodus 15:11*

I was in this large room crowded with people. On the other side of the room I saw my deceased husband Mike. He died March 15th, 2006. I tried to catch up with him, but couldn't. Finally he was out of my sight. I had a purse that was misplaced while I was trying to catch up with Mike. This purse was brown, old and worn. I tried frantically to find out where I had misplaced it, but to no avail. Later on I got a brand new black leather purse and was very pleased with it.

Interpretation

In the dream you were surrounded by people, which symbolize not being left alone in your grief, but still having active support and interaction with others. Seeing Mike (One who you esteem and love that is in heaven like God) but being unable to catch up with your deceased husband may symbolize the death of past hopes and dreams gone. This emphasizes the fact that you cannot return to the past no matter how much you miss Mike. (As Martha said to Jesus "by this time there will be a stench") The old purse also symbolizes a dated identity or the old 'wine skin'. Brown speaks of the death of Mike his natural organisms or body being without spirit, dried out and withered. In the dream you had suffered at a great depth from your great loss, exerted a lot of self-effort and you were 'worn' out. God has something new and better ahead for you!

The new black 'leather purse' is symbolic of your new 'wine skin', the new fresh anointing of the Lord. Black is a neutral color and it represents dusk. You are at the dawning of a new day, the midnight hour is over. You have experienced the mystery of death and overcome the grief from this physical affliction brought on by the loss of your soul mate. Your time of famine and mourning has ended. You will now be moved with a new passion. Leather is mentioned only once in the KJV of the Bible and it refers to a prophet. See *2 Kings 1:8, 'And they answered him, He was an hairy man, and girt with a girdle of leather about his loins. And he said, 'It is Elijah the Tishbite.'*

This new anointing will involve the prophetic (that views things as black or white) Word of the Lord coming to you in your life and you will be 'very pleased with it'. I believe the Lord is encouraging you to press forward in your walk with Him, as He has many new blessings in store for you! *Philippians 3:14, "I press toward the mark for the prize of the high calling of God in Christ Jesus."*

DREAM

Wake time: 7:00 a.m. *Daniel 7:5, "Arise and devour much meat!" Hosea 7:1, "For they deal falsely; the thief enters in, bandit's raid outside.*

Title: Creative Ten Times

I was on a bus in downtown. I had to get off at the crossroads store called 'Quality Meats'. I have been in this area in another dream, but never in real life. A man steals my wallet. I yell, 'get him'! A man comes out of store and runs after the thief. The thief turns and throws the wallet at me and then runs away. Next I'm in a house, telling friends I won't be around next year. I'm with people who have their faces painted royal blue. Somebody says, "It's not creative until it's been called that ten times."

Interpretation

Up to this point in your life you have been around a particular group of people. (bus) You have been heavily reliant on their influence for your spiritual and physical substance. Now you are coming to a crossroad where only meat, not the milk of the Word will satisfy. Somewhat like passing into the favor of spiritual maturity, desiring the deeper things of value and treasures from God. (wallet)

You may have experienced a situation where your identity in Christ has been attacked. You recognized what was happening and refuse the enemy's attempt to steal from you. Satan comes to steal, kill and destroy.

A house often refers to the life of the dreamer. Possibly the phrase, "I won't be around next year" could mean you will not be the same person a year from now that you are today. God is moving you onto a higher level of understanding. Eating quality meat will change you spiritually. The number ten means to nurture ordinal perfection and divine order to bring completeness in the fullness of time. It also means taking responsibility for God's law, His government which brings the trials of life and wilderness testing. When you have successfully passed through these tests you will experience a great restoration.

Blue faces would indicate healing, heavenly communion and revelation. Here the dream is saying you will meet people full of God's Holy Spirit, who will lead you into a greater knowledge of God's kingdom and ways. The world is perishing for the lack of knowledge of God. The church is starving for the lack of His presence. You have not seen Him as 'creative' yet, but you will. Unique things will happen in your life.

The dream is like a road map of your life. The enemy steals and you engage with others who help you recover and so on and on. God's Spirit will lead you into creative ways that will help assist others.

Let me invite you the reader to open a free online dream journal at www.MyOnar.com (Onar is the Greek word for dreams.) Then submit all of your dreams to me and my anointed skilled team of dream interpreters for an accurate dream interpretation that will be placed back in your very own private dream journal.

Lost Identity

Have you ever lost something in your dream? Usually the thing we lose is something that we are not able to replace, that we have borrowed, or is invaluable. People often lose their car (ego, ministry or vocation), keys (things you have been given ownership to), purse or wallet (personal credit or identity, valuables), a pet (friend, companion or something dear or loved), a child (inheritance, legacy, or spiritual fruit) or baby (an idea, something new) or a loved one (relationship). When purses or a wallet is lost it usually deals with a feeling of lost or stolen identity. The dreamer is in the process of recreating their image. They are in a transition of some type; leaving the old and stepping into a new beginning.

Women will dream of losing their purse when they are in a new relationship or starting a new career or an old relationship or career starts to take on a new appearance. She may be contemplating a divorce after many years of marriage. Or her children may be leaving for college and she is experiencing the empty nest syndrome. Who is she now? And more importantly who will she be after the divorce? What does she want out of life? What is important to her? How will others relate to her? When her new life begins to take shape and she is able to discover her new identity, the purse and all its belongings will reappear.

DREAM

Wake time: 6:00 a.m. *Proverbs 6:5, "Deliver yourself like a gazelle from the hunter's hand and like a bird from the hand of the fowler."*

Title: Black Birds in Purse

I was walking when all of a sudden there were five or six black birds flying out of my purse. When I saw the birds they startled me and I looked to see if there were more. There were two left inside my purse. So I tried to smash the black birds by swinging my purse violently against the wall. I heard a thump and knew they were dead. I was afraid to take them out, so I asked someone else to remove them from my purse. I asked them to check to make sure they were all gone.

Interpretation

A purse represents your identity. Birds can symbolize blessings or curses depending on their color and particular species. The fact that the birds scared you, were unwelcomed and black indicates a negative meaning. There were five or six birds. Five is the number of action, redemption and freedom. Six is the number of the weakness of man, toil, wrestling with the carnal and spiritual natures, incompleteness, the physical world or your humanity. Since the black birds came from your place of carrying money, possibly they could represent business deals or investments, which caused a financial or credibility loss. They also came out of your purse, which represents your identity. When you have killed these negative influences in your life, you will prosper and feel like a new person. The good part that should encourage you is the fact you hit your purse against the wall (a structure that gives support and also blocks advancement) and it stopped the continued loss. 'I asked someone else to remove them from my purse and to check to make sure they were all gone.' You will find or have found someone who will help you resolve these issues.

Lost Again

Some of us are born with great internal navigation systems. But, if you are like me, directionally challenged, you did not receive that wonderful gift. So you are like me, and so many others who would have a difficult time finding their way out of a paper bag. Recently, I was walking the beach alone talking to God about my life and pondering the plans He had for my future, when I realized I had forgotten to notice where the path was that led back to my friend's vacation condo.

This caused me to remember a time when I was lost on a beach as a child. I had wandered down the beach collecting seashells. When I looked up I was far away from the family's vacation spot. All of the hotels looked the same. I was not even sure which direction I should walk to get back. I would wander in one direction and then aimlessly wander back the other. I tried to be brave. I didn't want to cry. I walked and walked but nothing looked familiar. My little legs got so tired of walking. The heat of the sun made me thirsty and I was getting hungry.

Eventually I decided to walk up to an old couple who were reclining on the beach. I had passed them several times and they looked safe and loving. They were listening to a radio announcement about a little girl who was lost on the beach. They realized I must be that little girl. "Are you lost, little girl?" Just as they were trying to connect with me, Mom came running up the beach towards me. She looked like a panicked mother bear. When I saw her I ran to meet her. I began to cry. We collided into each other's arms. We both had a good cry as we celebrated my being found. Being lost in the natural and in our dreams is a fearful experience. Being lost can be terrifying.

No one plans on getting lost. We should all have goals or a planned objective. But we must remember that life is a journey, not a specific destination. We set our course with MapQuest or calibrate our destination in the GPS. But somehow something always seems to go wrong. In our dream an unexpected exit arises, a detour pops up to reroute us through an unknown city, or a policeman commands us to take the off ramp or issues us a speeding ticket or violation so we are not able to continue our trip as planned. All of these distractions cause us to be overwhelmed by fear. Confusion takes the place of good planning and we are left not knowing where we are or where we are supposed to be going.

When I first moved to Texas I got lost all the time, so my family gave me a deluxe GPS for Christmas. The most frequent phrase I heard was "recalculating!" A trip that should have taken me ten minutes turned into hours of driving on uncharted roads at breakneck speeds. I wondered if I would ever see my new home again. Would I even recognize my neighborhood since I was not familiar with the area? After all the convenience stores had closed I kept driving in circles until 2 o'clock in the morning. This was really bad news because I counted on the store clerks to help me navigate the next sector of new directions.

Finally, I spied an elderly man with his red tanker filling up the holding reservoirs of a gas station. I pulled off to road and skid to a stop to ask directions one more time. He offered that I was only ten minutes from home. I had been ten minutes from home all night. He was able to give me clear directions that set the correct course and led me home safely. What a relief.

It happens the same way in our dreams. We find ourselves lost, puzzled and bewildered. We continue asking directions, then we forget or confuse the directions we are given. We get more confounded and mixed up as the dream continues. Frustration and doubt continues to mount. Their weight makes it difficult to stay focused. We drive up the onramp, fly down the highway then take the exit ramp and try the feeder roads for a while. On again, off again, mile after mile we continue to circle on our endless journey never arriving and going nowhere fast. We are looking for love, security, purpose and happiness. We are sure that it will be right around the next bend in the road. None of the landmarks or road signs looks familiar.

There are so many things that continually vie for our attention and affections. Distractions come in many shapes and sizes. If we allow them to crowd us off God's desired course we can lose our direction in life. If we don't know our life purpose and destiny call, any road will lead us to a destination. But that destination won't be our highest or God's best for us. Our soul knows the essence or the fundamental nature of who we are called to be in life.

If we will listen to our dreams we will discover the right turns to take at the crossroads in life. Sometimes we must slow down to navigate the curves life throws at us. Often it is necessary to come to a complete standstill to seek God's face with all our hearts. Diligent prayer positions us to gain wisdom to properly navigate life's highways.

If we don't take our time while making important decisions, we can get off course. When we are sidetracked or off line, our dreams will show us finishing up on a dead-end street or being lost in a dark dangerous neighborhood. Will we give into fear and run? Will we get out of the hood with our lives? The only people available to ask directions are drug addicts, pimps and prostitutes who aimlessly crawl through the streets looking for their next fix or victim. No one in their right mind would exit the safety of their vehicle to ask directions from someone who is already lost. Has it come to this? Am I to get my life directions from dangerous strangers who have no direction of their own? The car is almost out of gas. No gasoline indicates we have used up the power that fuels resources. Without the proper assets and wisdom you cannot move forward. You need to find a gas station to refuel. Gasoline and oil lubricate the motions of the engine empowering all cylinders to fire, releases energy and ignites insights. The Holy Spirit is often pictured as oil or gas that ignites us with dunamis power and fire. The Holy Spirit propels us forward at great speeds to reach our purpose and accomplish our plans. The quantity or levels of these two symbols often represent our level of prayer, intimacy or anointing that empowers our lives to run smoothly. Without prayer or anointing we will not prosper or arrive at our destination.

Getting lost dreams are all about finding our safe place in life. They are about discovering our destiny by making the right life decisions that finally lead us home to a safe, nurturing environment. If you are lost in your dreams it is important to get focused. Spend time setting goals for yourself. Determine what is really important to you in life? What are your priorities now? What should your priorities be if you are going to reach your life goals, become happy and successful? What kind of changes do you need to make to bring safety, security and financial comfort into your life? What do you need to append to your life? And what do you need to eliminate? Remember this is your life not someone else's. You need to make these life-changing decisions by listening to your heart and soul. Ask God to guide you to make the best decisions to reach your highest potential.

Everyone you ask for advice will offer their opinion. Every opinion that is added only clouds the pool and stirs the water. In the end the only opinion and decision that matters is yours. Take some time to reflect on your real heart's desires and dreams. Then choose the high road, the narrow path, which is less followed to make your dreams come to pass.

Tornadoes Disaster Strikes

Tornadoes, hurricanes, tidal waves, tsunamis, and earthquakes are a few of nature's natural disasters that often strike in our darkest dreams. But what do they mean? When these powerful forces appear they usually represent some major changes, upheaval, devastation, trials, tribulation or destruction coming on life's horizon.

Tornadoes: represent changes in our emotional realm or physical geography or sphere of influence that changes the climate of our lives. There may be someone who continually loses their temper or has fits of anger and releases a verbal torrent of abuse in our presence. This creates an unwanted situation of anxiety, fear, confusion and a real turbulent emotional storm in our lives.

DREAM

Title: White Tornadoes

I was seated in a log home. I rose up to secure the building. I could see and hear a storm coming. I instantly knew it was Satan. He was coming to destroy me. I could feel his anger. I wasn't afraid but knew it was going to be a fierce storm. The storm was moving fast. There wasn't much time left. I looked to the sky and could see white tornadoes that were very clear and vivid. I counted seven white tornados and then they began to multiply. They were bright and very white. As I watched they ran into one other and exploded like Atom bombs.

Interpretation:

Your dream has many levels. A tornado can be good or bad depending on its color and the context of the dream. I have presented both aspects. This is a good dream.

Your dream speaks of upcoming events, which could include some last day events in which great power will be released from the heavens. It will be a time such as never before. God will pour out His Spirit upon mankind and great signs and wonders will follow.

The dream shows you in a relatively safe location spiritually. By standing on your foundation you will be in awe as you see the great events that will take place. The dream is to comfort you that even though you will feel the wrath of the enemy coming near you, you will also see the mighty power of God released on your behalf. *"And you shall know, understand, and realize that I am in the midst of Israel and that I the Lord am your God and there is none else. My people shall never be put to shame. And afterward I will pour out My Spirit upon all flesh; and your sons and your daughters shall prophesy, your old men shall dream dreams, your young men shall see visions. Even upon the menservants and upon the maidservants in those days will I pour out My Spirit. Joel 2:27–29 (Amplified Bible)"*

I was seated in a log home (old theology formed by leaders who are joined together built on a sturdy foundation). I rose up to secure the building (alert watchman). I could see and hear a storm coming (emotional turmoil; great mourning; commotion; transformation; warfare in the Spirit; judgment; sudden disaster or devastation; testing; trial at the hand of others; satanic activity; end times). I instantly knew it was Satan (spiritual discernment). He was coming to destroy me. I could feel his anger. I wasn't afraid but knew it was going to be a fierce storm. The storm was moving fast. There wasn't much time left. I looked to the sky (heavenward; my help comes from above, God) and could see white (God's power; revival; something God is bringing) tornadoes (strong powerful wind of change into your situation). I looked to the sky and could see white tornadoes that were very clear and vivid. I counted seven– (God's number of perfection, completion, fullness; seven also speaks of the seven spirits of God in *Isaiah 11:2* and *Revelation 4:5*) –white tornadoes and then they began to multiply (great increase revival brings multiplication *Acts 2:41* expand). They were bright and very white. (White speaks of the love of God and the Spirit of the Lord displaying His holy power and purity without mixture. White represents Christ, God's great light of righteousness and the holiness of God). As I watched they ran into one other and exploded like Atom bombs (great force and dunamis explosive power released through unity).

Second Interpretation

Again the storm headed towards you in your dream symbolizes Satan and his power. The white tornadoes symbolize the power of God headed towards you as well, and it clashed with Satan's power (storm) before it had a chance to slam into you, symbolizing God fighting for you.

Your fearlessness in this dream in the approaching storm symbolizes that your confidence is in God in real life. God has empowered you to keep cool and trust in Him to take care of you during the storms of life. God has always come through for you in the past.

The number seven symbolizes spiritual perfection. This means that through your times of waiting on the Lord to act on your behalf (symbolized by your counting to seven in your dream), He has done a work of spiritually perfecting your trust in Him. God has strengthened your perseverance during the storms of life.

White tornadoes symbolize the power of God bringing change in your life, shifting things into their proper places. The white tornadoes multiplying in your dream symbolizes that God may be multiplying the number of necessary changes in your life. These God changes will strengthen you and prepare you to fight in the days ahead. God wants to encourage you through this dream to continue to trust in Him (symbolized in your dream by your looking up to the sky for help, our help comes from the north or heaven) during these times of spiritual warfare! This dream may also be a call from God upon your life to become a spiritual warrior, as part of His army, to fight the spiritual battles headed your way! You have a powerful destiny in God.

He also wants to affirm to you that you are His son, He loves you very much, and He is proud of you! He loves utilizing you to fulfill His purposes and He will never abandon you (*Hebrews 13:5*) in the storms of life.

(See Dream Encounters Symbols Vol. I for a comprehensive list of Weather and Natural Elements Dream Symbols to use copyright 2010 www.BarbieBreathitt. com).

The Storms of Life

When problems and difficulties of any magnitude come crashing down on an individual, how do they escape or survive these destructive poundings? Is there a way of escape? These dreams of disaster strike without any warning. The disastrous storms of life destroy the existing leaders sweeping them away in a flood of water or the earthquakes and opens to swallow them up. They disappear without a moment's notice. The unsuspecting victims are left helpless and hopeless. Who will step up and take the lead? Where and when will the hero arrive to save the day? How will you be able to warn the people to escape before it is too late? What can be done to save these lives from certain death?

People who experience dreams about the storms of life usually operate in a high level of awareness of other people's needs, wants and desires. They are daring, dependable individuals who often shoulder a huge amount of responsibility. They carry duty far beyond the normal levels of accountability or what should be expected of them. They seem to rise to take the lead when everyone else loses hope or abandons the situation in fear. These heroes' are like CEO's who are able to see the big picture, find the way of escape, and bring a disastrous situation to a peaceful conclusion.

Dreams Reveal our Internal Questions, Talents & Treasures

Who am I? Who do I want to be when I grow up? What is my purpose and destiny in life? What are my gifts and talents? The answers to these and many other similar questions are found in our dreams. A correct dream interpretation leads us to discover who we were created to become in Christ. The questions we have about the future are answered in our dreams today. Our dreams reveal the essence of who we are or the underlying theme of our life.

We can trust God to supply the answers to life's enduring questions as we slumber by formulating dreams that bring the wanted insight to life's struggles. Our dreams are God's answers to the questions we hide within. When the dreams we dream answer life's questions and their wisdom is embraced we then have the courage to give them expression. The success we experience in our dream life can be transferred into our waking life. Dreams allow us to connect with who we are now but more importantly they form us into who we are called to become.

Dreams reveal the buried treasures that lay within each of us. Some dreamers have so many gifts, talents and abilities they appear as a treasure chest full of gold and precious stones in dreams. God has given each person unique gifts and talents that connect us to our world. No one can do the things you are called to do in life. You are the best and only you. The unique gifts and talents you possess enable you to help those who cross your path. Your life experiences and the wisdom you have gleaned becomes the answer to someone else's life. The skills you acquired to overcome life's disappointments can be shared with others to bring comfort and healing. Your pain was not in vain. God is able to take every painful situation and use it to reshape your nature. God can and will turn everything for your good.

Dreams answer questions and bring wisdom to solve difficult problems. They make us aware of how to break bad, perplexing habits and how to remove hindrances or obstacles that are keeping us from reaching our full potential.

Dreams give us creative solutions to problems we face in family or career relationships. Dreams unleash us into creativity and inventiveness. If we will grasp the new visions our dreams present, they will make us more open, flexible and attuned to our God-given abilities. We will be successful if we will only see things from God's perspective and make the necessary changes. If we don't take a chance or make any changes when answers are given to our questions, we will always come out with the same results. But, if we will allow our emotions to alert us that changes are needed, our dreams will give us the keys to a deeper understanding. They will unlock our aspirations, potential and destiny. Answers that are found in a correct dream interpretation bring healing to our brokenness by helping us to see the root system, which enables us to cut off their negative effects in our lives.

Warfare Dreams

Dreamers who are realists seem to always be at war in some dimension of their life. They view things from the far extremes of life and death, black or white, good or evil. It is hard for this type of person to compromise, see the grayscale or find any middle ground.

The realists are hardworking, loyal, protective friends if you are in their circle of influence. But, their philosophy in life is you are either for me or against me. You are on my team or you are a stranger and therefore an enemy or competition to be conquered.

Those who have frequent dreams of warring against enemies hold a high standard of excellence. They are always trying to overcome obstacles and breakthrough into a high level of success and productivity. They are creative innovators and entrepreneurs who see things the way they should be, 'Perfect!'

They are able to look at any person, plan or situation and see its flaws. They can be viewed as critical or judgmental. Their ability to see the big picture enables them to offer some ideas that will bring major improvements. They are high achievers and goal setters. However, once one goal is reached, several more must take its place. They are always striving with others, searching for the peace and happiness that seems to continually elude them. All real joy in life comes from the peace God gives that passes all of our natural understanding.

Realistic individuals flourish best in their own climate-controlled, secure, safe environment. They want to be in charge of everything because no one can do it to the standard of perfection they demand. Once they determine what has successfully worked in the past they have difficulty trying something new. They don't like to experiment with other's ideas without an assurance this new fangled technique or plan will supersede what they did in the past. Thus they are always warring to be heard, acknowledged and accepted, but they are not accepting of others.

The colors in warfare dreams are usually full of dark gray shades, black and white. The context of the dreams indicates someone or something is trying to capture, kill or destroy the dreamer or the things they hold dear. The dark strangers want to sabotage their carefully laid plans and strategies.

The images that appear in these dreams provoke a feeling of life threatening danger. Images of tornadoes, cyclones, tidal waves, sweep in from every angle. When the dreamers try to run quicksand, deep pits and jagged cliffs appear to prevent their escape. The enemy soldiers who invade with guns, knives, and tanks crowd into their demilitarized zone. The presence of these visionary war heroes' releases an internal strength that empowers you to run through a troop and leap over a wall. No weapon that is formed against you is able to prosper. (See Dream Encounters Symbols Vol. III for a comprehensive list of Spiritual and Military Weapons of War, to use copyright 2010 www.BarbieBreathitt.com).

Funeral Dreams

Have you ever attended your own funeral in your dream? I have. No matter whether the funeral is yours, or the funeral of a loved one; funerals conjure up deep feelings of finality, loss, grief, doom and despair. Are these dreams of death or dying indicators of a terminal illness or a death sentence? If you witness your own grave being dug or get to read the inscriptions on your grave stone it can be a warning to make sure your life is in order and that your will is current? It would be wise to make sure you have made peace with your Creator and you have secured heaven as your eternal resting place. To see your own grave can indicate that the numbers of your days are coming to an end. Salvation through Jesus is the most important decision you will make in life. If you do not have His eternal assurance that everything is well with your soul, do not rest until you make things right with God and man.

Although death dreams can indicate your time is coming to an end; most of the time seeing someone in their coffin or observing your own death, doesn't mean you are going to literally die. For the most part, death in a dream is a symbolic expression of something coming to an end. Death can represent a change, a loss of any number of things, such as a marriage, a friendship or relationship, a job, a career or a familiar support system. These funeral dreams indicate that something is dying or going through a drastic change never to return. A chapter in your life is drawing to a final close and a new chapter of promise will open.

When death appears in your dream, it is helpful to determine what area of your life has given destruction an open door. Are you killing someone or are you the one who is being killed? If you are the one who is dying in the dream this may be a positive indicator of a wonderful new beginning for you. The 'old negative you' is passing away and the 'new you' is being born again or will resurrect into a new exciting life.

Are you forming destructive or negative habits? Are your emotions out of control? Do you lose your temper, blow up or explode on friends? Are you killing yourself because you are not exercising self-control? Have you sold yourself out or died to your own dream of destiny or desires? No one considers death a friend. But if you will question why death has come into your dreams, you can lose the negative aspects of yourself. Bury them once and for all and resurrect the positive attributes of yourself and become a better person in the end. If you have engaged in self destructive bad habits, dropped your standards or developed negative behaviors, then those unhealthy, painful relationships need to die.

If you find yourself murdering someone, you are expressing your pent up rage in a most violent fashion. Is there someone in your life that is causing you an enormous amount of pain? Who is belittling or making fun of you? Is there someone who continually hurts your feelings or rejects you? Dying to self is a difficult, hard process because no one dies quietly.

Death, Trauma or Bereavement Dreams

The physical death of a loved one whether due to suicide, natural causes or an accident, is one of the most traumatic and painful experiences a person can face in life; second only to divorce with its continued assault of rejection and betrayal. At least with death there is a final closure, so the healing process can begin and finally be completed. But, often with divorce, the divorcee has to continue to relate to their ex-spouse on many levels, especially if little children are involved.

People relive these traumatic events over and over in their dreams. They experience the same feelings when the actual trauma took place. By feeling the pain, reliving the struggles and connecting with past or similar situations one's subconscious is able to help the dreamer process the pain and eventually the pain lessens.

Dream interpretation can help answer the myriads of questions we ask our friends and loved ones who remain. What is life about? Why did this have to happen? Why me? What did I do wrong? What could I have done differently? Did they ever really love me? However, sometimes our loved ones can only listen and offer their added support and concern. Sometimes it is necessary to seek out a kind, spiritual dream life coach to interpret the meanings of our dream messages or a professional counselor who can help us pray through to reach emotional health again.

Shame and Guilt Dreams

No one is perfect! But, does that mean we shouldn't try to be the best we can possibly be? We don't live in a perfect world, but wouldn't it be nice if we did? What would happen if everyone decided to be loving, kind and generous? What if we all treated people the way we wanted to be treated, with honor and respect? The world would be a much better place and we would all be happier too!

Life is about learning to give and receive love. The choices we make about whom, and how much we will or will not love, determines the quality of our today, and all of our tomorrows. Many of the difficult choices we make in life arise out of the powerful emotions of guilt and shame. Guilt comes because we have failed in some big or small way. We cheated big time on our taxes, stole something small, told a lie or maybe we exaggerated a lot to get ahead.

I attended a writer's conference where a ghost writer shared that her individual philosophy of life that gave her an edge or advantage over others, was to always exaggerate her personal and professional life by selling her image and skills as bigger than life, to make her sound better. This is not a philosophy I would ever adopt. To me, a person who sells themselves for a price is a prostitute. Who could ever really know or trust a person like that? It is so important to be truthful and honest in all our dealings. I personally would not pursue a relationship with a manipulative person that held to a belief which encouraged lies, exaggeration, overstatements and deception.

Have you ever noticed that when people talk behind their friend's back it is difficult for them to look them in the eyes? When confronted or asked, "Is something wrong?" They try to cover up their guilt with a little white lie or by sharing some juicy gossip about someone else. Remember, if they will gossip about that friend, or person they will gossip about you too!

Shame or guilt dreams come because we think we should have been able to do or say more than we were able to achieve. Shame dreams come when the legitimate needs of the dreamer are not validated. Guilt or shame dreams appear when people are devalued or made fun of by friends, family members or those he or she is in relationship with and or in close proximity to in the workplace, at home church, or in social settings. The soul invites us to take responsibility for our lives' decisions—good, bad and the ugly. Then when we are sorry for our mistakes, repent and ask God and others for forgiveness we are absolved of all guilt and shame.

These eye-opening dreams come to help us take responsibility for our erroneous actions. Shame and guilt dreams make it obvious that we need to confess our wrongs, sins and apologize. We clear our troubled consciences by telling the truth and setting the situation right by making amends. Once we have taken responsibility for the incorrect things we have done to someone else, we must take the next step and ask them to forgive us. A clear conscience will insure a peaceful night of sleep.

What if someone else is placing guilt or shame on you? Try to discern what your dream is telling you. Often the answers to resolving your problems are within the dream. How do you appear in the dream? Are you cowering like a little mouse in the corner of the room while your friend, spouse or boss is pictured as an elephant stomping through your house crashing every wall and boundary you attempt to erect? Are they knocking walls down trying to get to you because you have isolated yourself, due to fear or not wanting to communicate? Ask yourself why you are running away from problems or hiding. Why do you react this way? Is this a pattern of escape in your life? If it is, then what do you need to do to become a brave, bold confident lion or lioness? Determine what would help you gain some confidence and self-respect? Get rid of that timid, shy attitude; become bold! The righteous are as bold as lions. Begin roaring like a lion. You have value; your opinions and thoughts are important. Everyone deserves to be respected, complimented and honored. See this as an opportunity to explore your options, make a positive change, take on a new image and come out of your mouse hole.

Betrayal and Rejection

Rejection and betrayal take many forms. They are two of the most painful experiences anyone can live through. As a child you may have been the last one chosen to be part of the team. Your name was never called to come over in Red Rover, Red Rover. You were always left out or cast out once you got in. I was not a good reader in elementary school. I wanted to be in the 'Bluebird' reading group with all the smart kids, but my reading ability was not good enough. When I read my paragraph to try out for a new reading group the insensitive, calloused teacher let the whole class know that the highest group I could ever aspire to was the 'Black Crows,' or possibly the 'Busy Buzzards.'

Junior high wasn't much better. Between the raging hormones and the acne, no one wanted to be your friend. I dreaded shower time after physical education because I was a flat-chested, late developer. All the other girls with perky boobs proudly marched up to turn their tag over to show they had showered after recess.

However I struggled trying to make sure the hand towel covered every inch of my body so no one would notice my small breast. I also remember being devastated when the handsome art teacher I had developed a crush on humiliated me by asking in the crowded hallway, "Are you a boy or a girl?" I wanted to crawl into a hole somewhere and disappear.

No one wants to be exposed or to stand out in such a negative way. During those years when your peers noticed you or gave you some attention, it was usually to poke fun or to put you down to make themselves look better. I remember when they snickered and jeered at the uneven haircut I had received from Mom's loving hands at home. They laughed when my then fashion sense and creative flare sported a mismatched outfit comprised of multicolored stripes and various plaids, which would be considered very fashionable today.

Maybe, in high school you weren't chosen to be part of the service clubs, cheerleader squad, calendar girl or the homecoming court. If you were a late developer you weren't big enough to be on the football or wrestling team. Or you lacked the coordination required for tennis, baseball or the extra finances for the golf teams. If that was not disparaging enough, the homeroom teacher would not even acknowledge you when your hand was raised to ask a question.

In college you rushed the frat houses and fraternities, looking for love and acceptance, but none of them picked you. You've never been lucky in love or every meaningful relationship you have tried to develop continually ends in divorce or it fails time after time, leaving you with a broken heart. So now your shattered emotions are afraid to love again. Be encouraged! Man may have rejected you, but God will never reject you. You are God's special beloved and He delights in you.

Dream Title: The Runaway Bride

Date: 04/10/2010 *Song of Solomon 4:8–12,* "How beautiful is your love, my sister, my bride!"

Wake time: 8:23 a.m. *Revelation 18:23,* "And the light of a lamp will not shine in you any longer; and the voice of the bridegroom and bride will not be heard in you any longer; for your merchants were the great men of the earth, because all the nations were deceived by your sorcery.*

Waking Words of Ancient Wisdom Dream Symbol Card

Scripture verses for 8:23 a.m.

Your dream waking time was 8:23a.m. Using the Ancient Words of Waking Wisdom dream symbol card I looked up the various Scriptures for you to prayerfully consider how they could apply to your dream. God watches over His word to perform it.

Old Testament

Exodus 8:23, "I will put a division between My people and your people. Tomorrow this sign will occur."

Judges 8:23, "But Gideon said to them, "I will not rule over you, nor shall my son rule over you; the Lord shall rule over you."

1 Kings 8:23, "He said, "O Lord, the God of Israel, there is no God like You in heaven above or on earth beneath, keeping covenant and showing lovingkindness to Your servants who walk before You with all their heart."

Ezra 8:23, "So we fasted and sought our God concerning this matter, and He listened to our entreaty."

Proverbs 8:23, "From everlasting I was established, from the beginning, from the earliest times of the earth."

Zechariah 8:23, "Thus says the Lord of hosts, 'In those days ten men from all the nations will grasp the garment of a Jew, saying, "Let us go with you, for we have heard that God is with you."

New Testament

Matthew 8:23, "When He got into the boat, His disciples followed Him."

Mark 8:23, "Taking the blind man by the hand, He brought him out of the village; and after spitting on his eyes and laying His hands on him, He asked him, "Do you see anything?"

Luke 8:23, "But as they were sailing along He fell asleep; and a fierce gale of wind descended on the lake, and they began to be swamped and to be in dange

John 8:23, "And He was saying to them, "You are from below, I am from above; you are of this world, I am not of this world.".

Acts 8:23, "For I see that you are in the gall of bitterness and in the bondage of iniquity."

Romans 8:23, "And not only this, but also we ourselves, having the first fruits of the Spirit, even we ourselves groan within ourselves, waiting eagerly for our adoption as sons, the redemption of our body."

Dream: I'm running through the highways and byways trying to get away from the man I'm supposed to marry. I am looking for electrical wire. I end up at a tavern. I have to go through doors to get where I have to cross to the other side. The door keepers won't let me in because it's after 11 o'clock. I open the door anyway and there are a couple of guys I seem to know. They see me and laugh. I'm looking at myself as if in a mirror. I'm wearing the wedding dress I was married in. I run through the doors and down the steps outside. At the bottom of the steps, I sit at a table with my hand in cheek, feeling dejected.

Interpretation

This is what I hear "To run away or to hide away?" That is the question. A marriage speaks of a covenant commitment, an agreement that you are reluctant to engage in. Is there something that you are uncomfortable in committing to at work, in church, in your family or other relationships?

You were created to be with your Bridegroom and Lover. You are in search of His power (electrical wire) to save and deliver. You are looking for the sparks and fireworks of a passionate love! Jesus is the One who embraces all your attention and affection, never rejecting you, even when those around you may. Who is your first love? Reflect on God and obey the whispers of His voice which draw you out of vain imaginations and enveloping addictions, so you may increase and ascend in anointing and favor versus decreasing (going down steps). A cheek can refer to turning the other cheek. Holy Spirits presence surrounds you, His bride. He may close some eleventh hour doors for your protection because they will bring disorder and judgment.

Your dream took place on the twenty-fifth day of the month. Often, dreams that take place on this day require prayers of repentance and forgiveness of sin to bring a quick release and fulfillment of what is shown in the dream. If prayer is offered to God you should see the essence of God's grace moving on your behalf to bring you into a new training process.

> *Philippians 3:13–14, "Brethren, I do not regard myself as having laid hold of it yet; but one thing I do: forgetting what lies behind and reaching forward to what lies ahead, I press on toward the goal for the prize of the upward call of God in Christ Jesus." NASU*

Dream Title: The River

My family was going fishing, but they dropped me off at a campsite next to a river.

They said, "You can go in your own boat by yourself." I felt betrayed, left out and rejected. The campsite was pristine, very clean and orderly. One table had three shiny silver bowls on it. There was a fishing boat on its side against a tree for me. I turned to look at the river and was overwhelmed with delight to see how big, powerful and torrential it was. The water was a color blue that I had never seen before. It appeared between sapphire and turquoise. I just stood and stared at the river with excitement. Suddenly, I was in a tributary leading to the river, using a kickboard.

Dream with Interpretation

My family was going fishing [catch fish - winning the lost in life] , but they dropped me off at a campsite [temporary place in life] next to a river [move of God, Holy Spirit; prosperity of God's people; righteousness] and said "you can go in your own boat by yourself." [Learning to be spiritually self-sufficient] I felt left out. The campsite was pristine - very clean & orderly [organized]. One table had three [completeness & perfection- divine in nature] shiny silver [understanding; purity; cleanliness; redemption; words and promises of God] bowls [prepare; contain; store] on it. There was a fishing boat [individual ministry] on its side [not in use] against a tree [has roots and provides a covering for those of smaller stature] for me. I turned to look at the river & was overwhelmed with delight to see how big, powerful, torrential it was [eyes open to power of God]. The water was a color blue [revelation, heaven, divine, visitation, Holy Spirit, blessings] that I had never seen before - between sapphire [to judge, divine true judgment, execute righteousness, to rule, strive or strife, contend, the gift of discerning of spirits, work of perfection, eternal temple of God, testing, chosen, costly change in character and nature, the blue hue of the throne room in heaven, a living temple] & turquoise. I just stood and stared at the river [move of God] with excitement. Suddenly, I was in a tributary leading to [on the road to] the river, using a kickboard [not the boat? human power].

Interpretation

In your dream, your family going fishing at a campsite represents a time of refreshment and relaxation that is coming. When your family suggested you go fishing by yourself you felt left out. You felt like you were rejected by those who should be able to offer you the most support and comfort in life. When people reject us we turn to God for support and comfort. He never disappoints. God is doing something new in your life. *"Behold, I have made all things new." Revelation 21:5*

God often uses those who are close to us to bring about His plans and purposes. Sometimes the people who know us the best don't readily understand or appreciate us like they should. The result of their rejecting you caused you to branch out on your own. You needed to discover who you are and what you are capable of accomplishing. You were being separated to explore a new area in your own life. Their rejection may have caused you to feel alone in your life's journey or experiences with God. We all journey through life alone to some extent. Your family was unable to fully share in the joys of your intimate relationship with God.

The big, powerful, and torrential river in your dream represents a big, powerful, and flowing move of the Holy Spirit. The Holy Spirit is already 'flowing' like a river throughout the earth. Since you have a hunger for more of God, God has invited you to 'jump in' and enjoy going with the flow of the Holy Spirit in your life! You have much to contribute! [tributary]

The color silver symbolizes 'redemption' and the number three symbolizes 'complete'. The bowls symbolize the 'bowls of wrath' containing life's harsh circumstances in your life from the past. So the three silver bowls are God's way of telling you that He is going to completely redeem all of the 'harsh circumstances' in your past. One way that you can receive that complete restoration and redemption is by simply jumping into the river (Holy Spirit) and having fun in Him (symbolized by going into the water with a kickboard)! The river of the Holy Spirit will also 'wash' all of the painful memories and hurts away from your life.

Your dream shows the Lord moving you into a time of learning of Him and His truths alone. The Lord has prepared and ordered this time of learning and growing in Him. He will be bringing someone [Holy Spirit] into your life to help guide you into who He wants you to be. He will help you gain the knowledge to be of service to the Lord. The Lord wants to use you to help others come to a better understanding of the Divine nature and who He really is.

> Lean on, trust in, and be confident in the Lord with all your heart and mind and do not rely on your own insight or understanding. In all your ways know, recognize, and acknowledge Him and He will direct and make straight and plain your paths. Proverbs 3:5–6 (Amplified Bible)

Sometimes the pain of rejection and betrayal is so extreme it hurts to breathe. It feels like you won't live through the day. The realization that someone you have trusted, loved, shared your life and secrets with has turned on you like a ravenous wolf is more than one can tolerate.

If you allow negative thoughts to occupy your mind their destructive actions can destroy your emotions. You are left with a sober truth of rejection having struck again. Betrayal grips your throat like a hangman's noose made of rough, dry rope. As you are suspended in midair you swing from one negative emotion to another, it's difficult to find any stability.

You may ask, "Why do rejection and betrayal seem to be my only constant friends and dreaded companions?" "What is wrong with me?" "Am I a bad person?" or "Is this my portion in life?" "How do I break and get out of this devastating cycle and downward spiral?" "How do I find true love, respect and acceptance?" God is the answer to all of life's problems. Surrender your pain and the ashes of life to Him. Ask the Holy Spirit to exchange your ashes for His beauty and give you the needed wisdom to overcome these challenges.

Dream Title: Insecure

I walked into a theater. My husband was sitting with a girl who is our neighbor. I sat down behind them. The girl had her head on my husband's shoulder. She turned to me and told me that she and her husband fight all the time. She said that she needed my husband. The only thing I remember was just the two of them. It seemed like they were in the back of the theater. I don't remember anything else in the dream except I do remember seeing something red in the background. I have had reoccurring dreams of my husband with other females but they are always in different scenes.

You have interpreted the dream in the title you gave it, 'Insecure.' Holy Spirit is bringing to the forefront of you mind feelings that need your attention. These negative feelings can produce destructive power that can damage or even destroy relationships and self-esteem.

Luke 5:22 "But when Jesus perceived their thoughts, He answered and said to them, "Why are you reasoning in your hearts..." Could it be that God is telling you to change the way you think about yourself? Your husband in the dreams could be a symbol of self-rejection. *Proverbs 23:7 For as a man thinks in his heart, so is he.* Everything becomes as we sees it.

Your dream is exposing insecurity about your own value. You feel as if you are taking a backseat to other women. God wants to reinforce His love for you. Whenever you doubt God's love or the love of your husband, which could make you see the color red, for anger, it is wise to remember God's passion for you, which is also represented by the color red. I do not believe this is a literal dream about your husband being unfaithful. Be true to and love yourself. You have great value to those around you. This woman wanted to have a loving relationship like you and your husband have.

Theaters allow us to view things that are and are not taking place in real life. The setting suggests that dark thought patterns are at work here. Many attractions or distractions will try to steal your assurance that God or your husband is faithful. Disappointments or struggles will seem at times to tip the scales against knowing you are favored (the girl who says she fought with her husband - girls are immature and childish). God dialogued with you in this dream; He does not want you to give heed to setbacks.

Also, when you see God favoring other people, it does not mean that it takes away from His passion towards you.

"In a desert land he found him, in a barren and howling waste. He shielded him and cared for him; he guarded him as the apple of his eye." Deuteronomy 32:10

People, who have experienced a lot of rejection or betrayal throughout their lives, if they have not let go, stopped trying and given up, hold relationships in high regard. They are intelligent, sacrificial givers, very kind and extremely loyal people. They will often border on becoming the martyr because they will relinquish their wants and desires to please others. They know the pain of rejection, so they try to protect those around them from ever experiencing that pain. They will go to the extremes to insure they never knowingly treat anyone in the unjust way they have been treated.

They become the peacemakers who bring synchronization to the overall whole so things remain harmonious at the office, home or with friends. They are the first to submit. They give up their rights or opinions to go along with what the majority wants. They feel maintaining peace and meeting other's needs or desires is more important than speaking out or standing up for what they really want. You hear them say, "Oh I don't know?" "Whatever you think or want." "It really doesn't matter to me; I'm happy just to be a part of what you are doing." When in reality what they think, desire and want matters a great deal. Because they do not stand up for themselves or give themselves any value because they are constantly giving in, people stop giving them honor and respect, and eventually reject them.

Dream Title: A Man of My Past (Reoccurring Dream)

Date: May 1, 2010

Waking time: 6:00 a.m.

I keep having a dream about a man from my past that rejected me. Each time I dream about him we are always talking on the phone. We talk about the past and how he rejected me. I was telling him how he told me to stop calling him and I did, and he said no-o-o, very sadly. I have this dream often, but the conversation is always different but always about the past. We do not talk on the phone at all.

One time I had a dream about him in March; that I was asking him a question about something and he called four days later.

Interpretation

The dream reflects an issue of rejection that you have not fully surrendered to God. God is telling you over and over in your dreams you must forgive and surrender it to Him. God knows the damage this sort of rejection can do to a woman emotionally if it is not dealt with on a spiritual level. Jesus was rejected by all of Jerusalem and fully forgave them and us. God wants you to follow the example of Jesus for your own sake. Your soul will continue to give you this dream until the message is received. This is why the dream is repeating the message over and over again. The number four (4 days) symbolizes God's creative works (or weakness) which can and will set you free from this emotional harassment.

Also this recurrent dream indicates that there are soul ties with this man of your past. By him calling you, and you wanting him to stop conversations, shows that there are some residual control issues from your past.

The dream is telling you this man has been influential in the way you think or perceive things, but that you are unable to make the clear cut you wish for. You are still struggling with feelings of rejection. The Creator is exposing them so you can take steps to be free from these hurtful, restraining, controlling thoughts.

The dream implies that staying in that place of rigid patterns (month of March is number Gimel (3) perfect witness, union, fullness and life) will affect your spiritual walk and leave you weak (number Dalet (4) means also weakness). This dream is encouraging you to break free! It shows the care and concern of a loving God! Your wake up time (6 a.m.) six is the number of man, with his limited wisdom. Dreams that take place on the first day of the month, come to bring delight and happiness. They deal with God's sovereignty. God is releasing a new beginning to you by bringing a unity or link between heaven's plans for your life and your present earthly reality.

Inner Vows

Everyone experiences rejection at some level in life from time to time. Rejection can be an indicator that it is time to move on to bigger and better things. I worked for an organization where I continually experienced rejection and betrayal. I had to learn to hold onto things very loosely because they would give a measure of authority or a small promotion and then snatch it away. Their leadership styles were controlling, harsh, judgmental, cruel and opinionated, never complimenting anyone, but only criticizing their every effort to please. Nothing anyone on staff did was ever good enough. Once I left that organization I adopted an internal policy. I decided I would never treat the people who worked with me the way I had been treated. I would do things the exact opposite way. I'd be open, empowering, giving, caring, inclusive and encouraging.

It is important to stay away from making vows against never rejecting others. "I will never treat anyone the way they treated me!" "I will always go the extra mile, be a good listener and friend." If we adopt these life philosophies we may mean well but we may eventually find ourselves being surrounded by gripers and complainers who are nonproductive and suck every bit of life's energy right out of us. True, we should not take up someone's harmful, hurtful actions or unleash the things we have suffered on others. We all know that paralyzing pain. It is important to retain and share the wisdom we have received through the trials of life.

Give love, grace and mercy where it is needed. But don't become a soft, wishy-washy, man pleaser who facilitates other's wants and wishes to the point that your total acceptance causes you to be lost in the equation. People who are controlling and selfish always try to make every situation about them. I want this or I want that. Giving into their tantrums, rage and self-centered controlling demands is not good for them and only harms you. You are important and you do matter! It takes courage to accept and love yourself as well as others. Your happiness is vital and necessary.

When I started dating I was afraid to tell my date what I wanted to do or where I wanted to go. When my date asked, "What do you want to do?" I was afraid I would choose the wrong place or somewhere that was out of his budget. So my response was "It doesn't matter to me, you choose." I would not even offer any suggestions. Then my mother told me, "It is important to have an opinion and state what you desire of life. If your date asks you where you want to go eat, tell him." "If he can't afford where you want to go, he can advise you and offer another choice or save his money until he can take you where your heart desires. Remember, what you want out of life is important!"

Got the Job!

Rejection is not always negative. If we always settle for less, when we could have more or the best, we will always have less. One morning mom met me in the kitchen. She said, "I had a vision about you last night. Hurry up, get dressed you are going to interview at Scott Lake Elementary this morning for the kindergarten position." I responded, "Really! Tell me the dream." Mom said, "I saw a single file line of teachers with resumes in hand that led to the principal, Mr. Byrd's office. The line of teachers streamed all the way through the parking lot and out to the highway. I saw you at the end of the line. But suddenly another door opened up. You were escorted to the front of the line, past all the other teachers who were waiting. You were given great favor. You became the head instead of the tail. You are going to get this job today!"

When I interviewed for my first teaching position there were fifty-four applicants for one job opening. I had just graduated from Southeastern University with honors, but had no teaching experience. Scott Lake Elementary was the best school in the county and a lot of teachers with seniority were determined to get that position. I threw my resume in with the rest of the applicants and hoped for the best.

Promotion, grace and favor come from God and so do open doors. I could have very easily allowed the fear of rejection to stop me from applying or interviewing. There were so many who had experience and some were already experts in the teaching field. That day fifty-three people experienced rejection, but I didn't. Because I acted on mother's vision, I was rewarded the kindergarten teaching position. I was at that school for sixteen years and got to touch the lives of hundreds of children every day.

Life is full of painful situations, disappointments and learning experiences. The beautician has to trim the dried ends off their client's hair or the hair will continue to break and look awful. The Chef must choose the best ingredients and discard the rest or his dish will not meet the standard of excellence. A surgeon uses a scalpel or a laser light beam to cut away things that can harm their patient. Critical words can cut like a knife, but a critique done in love will help us grow and flourish.

The potter's hand must cut the marred, air-filled lumps of clay from the vessel she is creating. She must cast the hard lumps clay back into the water until they are soft enough to mold. Then she pounds, folds and beats the clay with her skillful hands until all the air bubbles are removed. Then and only then is that lump of clay fit to be part of the whole. Once the clay has gone through the preparation process it can easily be molded and flows like smooth silk onto the vessel. The redesigned vessel is placed in the fire to cure and harden. Lastly, it is painted and then re-fired once again to be sealed for purpose. So it is in our lives. We must go through the process to become a beautiful, useful vessel of honor. When we have emptied ourselves the Holy Spirit rushes in to fill us to overflowing with His presence and power.

People who have suffered through years of rejection and pressed through betrayal usually develop a spirit of excellence. They quietly do their best but seldom ask for or receive any thanks or recognition. They develop a witty sense of humor because they have experienced so many disappointments in life. To cope with their pain they learn to laugh at themselves, use sarcasm or crack jokes. The laughter has acted like a medicine to sooth the unbelievable emotional hurts, sorrow and grief they have encountered. They focus on and see the silver lining as grace that frames the dark cloud that has overshadowed their lives. They are determined individuals who are able to complete a task, scale the wall, or run the race to win no matter how many obstacles arise against them.

Overcoming Rejection

Dream Title: Race

Date: April 7, (4:7) 2 Timothy 4:7

I was at the beginning of a race. I had no legs, but stubs with skates. The other racers had their legs. The racers and the crowd of people jeered at me, because I was determined to race and finish anyway!! I took off and push hard on my hands, then arms, then elbows! The others finished way ahead of me! The crowd just stared at me and wondered why I was even bothering! Against all the odds being against me, I kept going, determined to finish! Then one person started clapping, then another, then another, till finally, they all were applauding me, rooting for me to just finish. It was as if their eyes were opened and they could finally see why I was racing! Then I woke up, but knew once I did finish the race, something big and awesome was going to happen!

Interpretation

"I have fought the good fight, I have finished the course, I have kept the faith; in the future there is laid up for me the crown of righteousness, which the Lord, the righteous Judge, will award to me on that day; and not only to me, but also to all who have loved His appearing." 2 Timothy 4:7–8 NASU

God is trying to encourage you with this verse, through your dream! In your dream, you were at a great disadvantage compared to the other racers because you had no feet. It symbolizes that you may feel that you do not have a leg to stand on or that things have happened to you in the past that may put you at a disadvantage compared to other people. But in your dream, it didn't matter what people thought; all you cared about was finishing the race well! This is very admirable so many begin and race or put their hand to the plow, but do not finish well.

The race can symbolize your destiny in God, which means that in real life you are focusing on fulfilling your destiny in God regardless of the 'odds' working against you. Even if people do not initially believe that you can fulfill your destiny because of things that have happened to you in the past, they will eventually take notice when they see your love and perseverance in Christ! They will cheer you on and you will inspire them, just as you saw in your dream! God believes in you, and we believe in you too! God wants you to know that you will finish your 'race' in real life, by fulfilling your destiny in Him! Your Heavenly Father is proud of you, His precious beloved daughter! He is always cheering you on. *"Blessed is a man who perseveres under trial; for once he has been approved, he will receive the crown of life which the Lord has promised to those who love Him." James 1:12 NASU*

This dream proves that God loves you very much. You are the apple of His eye. It is His gentleness that makes you great. He collects every tear you have cried. The journey for you has been long and hard. Your spirit is willing but your flesh has been weak.

This dream marks your spiritual journey to maturity. Your wounding has been great. The Lord says that you are not responsible for your wounding, but you are responsible to open your heart, so He can lead you to total recovery. Your heart has been to love and not hurt people. You have persevered despite being jeered at, rejected, criticized and mocked because of your faith not lining up with your actions. You have not quit despite the whispers of the enemy for you to just give up. The Word of God says a bent reed He will not break. God is faithful. He has met you where you are in your time of need. He has chased you down and hedged you in *Hosea 2:6,* despite you breaking through the hedge many times; He has pursued you with His mercy and goodness, *Psalms 23*.

God wants to give you the revelation that you are able to trust Him because His cross proved that He has your best interest at heart. This revelation Ephesians 1: 16–21 will bring healing to your heart in the area of broken trust. You are an overcomer. The Holy Spirit has great things for you so that you can be a blessing and inspiration to others. God will use all things to form and fashion you. Nothing will be wasted, nothing!

This dream may be giving you evidence that you have taken on a venture, ministry or project of some sort for which you have no support system, no legs. You find it difficult because the negative words others speak about your endeavor. Tenacity holds you to your course or race. The dream is to encourage you not to give up; because victory lies ahead, along with adulations from those who thought you could never accomplish your goal.

Acceptance is not always the best policy. Often the choices we make today come from the strong feelings generated by rejection or betrayal. The all too famous should have, could have, and would have's, begin to take over our thinking processes, filling us with regrets. I should have said more, done more or I could have said it differently.

Rejection dreams come when the legitimate needs of the dreamer are not validated. When an opinion is shared in a social setting, in the home or workplace, people devalue it or, worse yet, make fun of your input. The soul invites us to take responsibility for our lives' decisions—good, bad and ugly. Our input and opinions are important; by valuing ourselves we can be absolved of all rejection.

It's okay to reject people who only follow their own selfish agendas; they will never have your best interest at heart only their opinions and feelings matter. It's all about them. They constantly force their will upon you, in no way considering your wants or desires. They continually hurt, intimidate and abuse you. They are trying to press you into their mold, to control you, insuring you serve their plan? You are not their cute little poodle on a leash that has no choice but to follow whatever they say, do what they do, or go wherever they go. You are not a trained puppet on a string who responds to their every desire with, "Yes, Whatever you want dear!" Remember you are a valuable individual with your own personality, calling, vision and desires. Learn to confront in love. Establish safe boundaries and speak up. Learn to set high goals for yourself and then make a plan of action to insure you achieve those goals. Stop allowing others, especially family members, to selfishly control your life and happiness.

Chapter 9
Common Dreams and Dream Symbols

Elevators: reflect our current level of progress with a question or problem we are experiencing in life. An upward motion represents increase and a positive promotion while a downward movement indicates a decrease or demotion is coming.

The working condition of and the direction the elevator is moving tells us a lot about our situation. Is the elevator malfunctioning, moving sideways or crashing through the floors? Is it shooting sky high but stopping on the wrong floor so we never reach our destination? Sometimes the elevator is frozen and won't move or we are trapped in transition between floors and can't get any assistance to free us from the prison within the elevator's four walls.

A woman shared a dream she had of the elevator in her apartment building not working. In her dream she wanted to move out of her apartment into another apartment on a higher floor. But every time she packed up or planned to move the elevator would break. Each time the elevator broke she reported the malfunction to the administration in the lobby. The administration would suggest what changes needed to happen to enable her to side step these issues and move higher, but she never addressed the problems; so they were never corrected. It became a frustrating cycle that continued to limit her forward progress.

This dream indicated that the dreamer had a desire to be successful and move up into a higher place of influence. But she was not willing to make the administrative changes that were necessary to allow this promotion or increased level of exposure to take place in her life. The dream indicated some character issue that kept coming to light. She was willing to talk about them, and to blame others for her limitations, but she continually refused to take the necessary steps to illuminate them from her way of conducting business.

Malfunctioning elevators can be very frustrating because they hinder us from reaching our purpose, desired level of exposure or influence. They can plunge towards the ground to crash at great speeds. A broken elevator can slow or totally stop our progress by making us feel out of control or disconnected from our goals.

When we are trapped on an elevator that is plummeting to the ground we are left with a feeling of hopeless failure and great disappointment from something that has let us down.

This is a wakeup call to take steps to correct the areas in your life that need to be fixed by being honest with yourself. Honesty is always the best policy because it can get you back on track to obtain victory and favor. Stop pretending nothing is wrong. Be willing to face the negative facts and make changes that will cause you to prosper and rise to a new level of success.

Elevators travel up and down in the same pattern continually. If we want to change the pattern our elevator is following we must adjust our attitudes to reflect an upward, positive outlook on life.

DREAM:

I am at an expensive hotel. I get on an elevator and a man gets on with me. We are the only two on the elevator. I am holding a toddler. We are going to the 21st floor, which is the top floor; apparently this is where he is staying. I notice that he has a small slight birthmark on his left temple. The elevator is going VERY fast. I realize that the man is Satan and I get scared. Then all of a sudden I am not scared any more and I notice that he is nervous and I sense he wants to get off the elevator.

Interpretation:

Satan lives in SIN which is represented by the number (twenty one, which means exceeding sinfulness). Satan wants all of us to be dependent upon him or join him. You are holding a toddler (a young gift that is developing and learning to walk but is not yet totally sufficient or balanced). Satan wants to take us to the height of sin as FAST as possible (twenty first floor). But, the good news is that on the way, revelation comes of how sin can 'mark' our thinking, dirty our temple, weaken our faith (left), and destroy the destiny that we were born to walk in here on the earth (birthmark on left temple; the mark can also represent the mark of the beast Revelation 16:2)...when we carry the fear of God, the enemy is scared of the holy power within us and he will flee..... *"Submit yourselves therefore to God. Resist the devil, and he will flee from you," James 4:7* (on elevator, after fear left you, Satan became nervous and fearful and wanted to get off the elevator). When sin is discovered, repented of, and then removed from our lives, we become a dangerous threat to Satan's kingdom of sin and darkness. *"Do you not know that your body is the temple (the very sanctuary) of the Holy Spirit Who lives within you, whom you have received [as a Gift] from God? You are not your own, you were bought with a price [purchased with a preciousness and paid for, made His own]. So then, honor God and bring glory to Him in your body." 1 Corinthians 6:19–20*

Submission to God takes you higher and increases favor and anointing (going up in an elevator)...blessings... Our body is to be the Holy Temple, the dwelling place of God.

Guns: are threats of aggressive energy being used against someone in a powerful or forceful manner by a particular person who wants to do harm. Guns represent someone who is shooting off at the mouth or fiery, hateful, harmful or murderous words of abuse or accusation that are able to travel a long distance to reach someone at an incredibly accelerated speed. But at times the gunner could be your own personality that is sticking up for you and your wants, opinions or desires in a situation; remember the term "Sticking to your guns."

Knives: represents stabbing, hurtful or cutting words that cause us to feel isolated or separated from romance, friends, family members or those we associate with in other areas of our lives. These cutting remarks slice away, leaving us with deep, gashing wounds that continue to fester as our very life's blood seems to flow out of us. As a result of these caustic words we feel powerless and drained of our life's energy force. When women dream about knives, it more often than not relates to some type of emotional hurt from a man who is pursuing them for a sexual relationship. When men dream of knives, they are usually in some type of hand to hand combat or competition at work or in sports with another person and the weapon of choice is a knife.

TEETH

Teeth represent dependability and acting consistently with our foundational up-bringing and morals, loyalty to our personal values, faithfulness to our belief systems, remaining in a state of trustworthiness or truthfulness towards ourselves and others.

We will often experience our teeth becoming loose (warning of unfaithful friends), decaying or falling out (fear of losing your looks, sex appeal or attractiveness through the aging process) when we are compromising on our morals, principals or our foundational belief system in some area of our lives. Our dream mechanisms let us know we are paying too high of a price to seek someone's favor by adjusting to or lowering the standard we have always upheld.

Molar teeth can also represent our ability to mold or remold something trying to gain understanding, as we mull over (molar) it or chew on the facts for a while. The need of wisdom comes into play when the wisdom teeth appear in a dream. Baby teeth represent immaturity, childishness, limited wisdom or knowledge, a lack of experience or that a person is free from corruption. Incisors represent stress and worry that causes indecision when sorting through the issues of life. Pray for wisdom and peace to make correct decisions. Wrong decisions will lead to regret and extreme abhorrence, while a correct decision will lead to abundant blessings. Eye teeth can represent a prophetic or seer gift where revelation knowledge comes in the form of a vision or dream.

The teeth of an animal represent something that is penetrating your boundaries of resistance. Animal teeth indicate a clever, crafty, and cunning presence that has a real danger of devouring you through caustic words that have a nasty bite to them. Long sharp teeth represent a false friend or an enemy involving you in legal actions.

Broken teeth indicate a contrary process or issue that will lead to a broken relationship if proper steps are not taken to prevent this loss. Teeth that are worn means there is an enemy who is busy at work wearing on one of your close relationships. Their words are forming spears and arrows that destroy. Teeth that are broken foretell of learning obedience through suffering from affliction *Job 4:10*. A dental bridge is a warning to structure your life better. Choose words that build up, instead of always being critical or tearing people down with your words. If you are toothless it means you are lacking force or the ability to bite down or discern circumstances; you are suffering from a lack of wisdom.

To see yourself brushing your teeth in a dream means it is very important to clean up the way you speak in order to remove obstacles that have stained your reputation; take care in thoughtfully choosing the right words. If you are wearing false teeth, be careful not to exchange spiritual knowledge, wisdom and understanding for human reasoning, traditions and error.

To dream of a toothache represents an affliction, a quarrel and backbiting or a trial that is coming. If the void or cavity is not filled in time, it will lead to heartache, disappointment, sorrow and pain. Decay indicates a health problem or gossip and bitter envy that rot the bones. In contrast white beautiful teeth bring happiness, health and prosperity.

DREAM Title: Tall Dark and Handsome

A woman shared her dream. I keep having these reoccurring dreams of different tall, young handsome men kissing me on my lips (mouth). They seem about fifteen or so years younger than me. One of the men had very white teeth with spaces between them. These men are unknown to me and are always tender, loving and seems as though they want to help me.

In one of my dreams, the young man was a well-known actor and singer, and in the dream the Holy Spirit said, "Tell him you love him", I did and he quickly reciprocated.

Interpretation

Your reoccurring dream is about you receiving the love, affection and tenderness (symbolized by a kiss) of Jesus in different ways, as symbolized by the different tall, handsome men in your dream. Each man's tall and handsome features are God's symbolic way of wooing or attracting you to Himself.

The number fifteen symbolizes the energy of divine grace, resurrection in glory, deity, rest, mercy and deliverance from death, but it especially represents the bride of Christ for you (*Ephesians 5:25–27*). You are part of the Bride of Christ (the Church)! Jesus the Bridegroom is wooing you and sealing His spiritual union with you as His "bride" through kisses. As you received each kiss from Jesus, His love was imparted to you; when you told the celebrity that you loved him, he reciprocated because he was changed by the love of Jesus in you. Jesus is giving you this dream over and over again because He will not stop romancing you, His precious bride! As you continue to receive the love, affection and tenderness of Jesus' kisses, His love in you will change the people around you.

DREAM Title: All I Want for Christmas is my Two Front Teeth

In my dream it was as if I was watching something, not sure what I was watching or where I was. I suddenly realized I had two of my front upper set of teeth in my hand. I was looking at them. I then swirled my tongue in my mouth looking for the missing teeth, but there were none missing. Where I thought they were missing I still had the teeth. It was as if I had new teeth. End of dream. After waking and thinking about the dream I had sensed something about cutting new teeth came to mind.

Interpretation

In the dream you were watching something. This phrase could indicate something is happening in your life that you do not understand the what, when, where or why of it.

The tongue holds the power of life and death in it so choose your words wisely. Teeth can represent understanding and comprehension or the use of the mouth in blessing or cursing. New teeth may be a new way of talking or speaking, communicating blessings or new decisions that need to be made. Be careful not to 'bite too much off' when starting a new project. Work your way into it slowly so you don't become overwhelmed. Watch your words because they have the power to create.

If you are 'cutting new teeth' you will be learning new important truths. The dream is telling you that you will receive the insight and understanding needed to fulfill the plans God has for you.

Chapter 10
People are Significant

The people that are in our lives are extremely important. Some of the relationships we develop with them will change our lives forever. Sometimes these changes are for our good. But, sometimes these changes are damaging and the relationship is harmful. One would expect to dream about their lovers, family members, friends and work associates because we interact with them on a daily basis. But why do people we have never met or hardly even know appear in our dream scripts at night? Why do childhood bullies appear haunting us in our sleep? Could it be there is someone in our waking life that reminds us of the feelings we had long ago? Why does the sweet neighbor girl you had a crush on come strolling by with her blonde hair flowing in the wind? Is she still available? Is it possible you could still connect? Why do people who are no longer in our lives suddenly reappear in our dreams? Why do those who have crossed over into death spring back to life in the visions of the night? These same people continually visit us night after night, acting out their pre-described roles. But why are they there? Why was this particular person chosen to be cast in that particular role at this time? What do that person's occupation, character traits, talents and position in life mean to you?

Often people in our dreams represent someone we admire or look up to. We secretly wish we could be like them. We want to be as pretty as they are or as smart as they appear to be. We respect their status, opinions or belief systems. Sometimes the people who appear in our dreams remind us of a former time or history in our lives. That person reminds us of the appropriate or inappropriate responses, emotional feelings or decision making processes that took place. The particular person in our dream stimulates our emotional feelings. We associate them with the feelings we experienced when we knew them. They may remind us of hope, joy and good times or fear, despair, hopelessness or trauma. But invariably their dream presence will provoke some type of feeling, response or emotion in us. If our dreams are reintroducing a deceitful person from the past it is a warning to be evaluate ones current relationships.

People who have suffered through the pain of divorce will dream of their former partner when they begin to experience the same type of romantic feelings or emotions in their current relationship. The ex-wife from hell may appear as a tigress pouncing on the families closed door, throwing her weight around to claw her way back into your life through the dreams of the night. She may be smoking, cursing, threatening to ruin your reputation, while exposing her breast or wearing seductive clothing, like a prostitute, to lure or blackmail you back under her powers. For women, your irresponsible drunk of a husband, who gambled his paychecks and could never keep a job, will begin to sabotage your present happiness by bringing the weight of his debt crashing down on you. The appearance of these negative people symbol types in dreams act as signal symbols; they alert us to pay attention because something is wrong.

People, who have caused pain in the past, will revisit in our dreams, if we are relating to people in our present, in the same way we did in the past. If we start experiencing those same types of emotional pain or fears these painful figures from our past will reappear. They let you know that you may be falling back into the negative patterns of the past. You may be repeating a toxic prototype association or making a mistake being involved in the same type relationship.

Are you allowing past fears to haunt and intimidate you again? Evaluate where you are in your life and relationship. Ask yourself, "Why am I withdrawing or feeling these same fears again?" Then make the necessary changes to correct the state of affairs. Don't allow yourself to repeat old harmful patterns. Break out of the cycle and respond in an opposite, positive manner. Don't allow those negative characters to have any power in your present situation. They stole your happiness once; don't allow them the power or access to your thought life to do it again. You deserve to be happy and fulfilled.

When people visit us in our dreams, they can also be imparting positive things such as wisdom and spiritual gifts to us. We are able to glean from their example and actions. Their various abilities or the talents they carry can be received by us when they appear in our dream sphere.

Some dreams, especially those that are close to the vision realm, are so real the actions and situations that take place in them are recorded by our brains as actual physical events. Our brain receives the dream and records the details forming a new pattern, script or plan we will be able to follow as we bring them to memory. We are able to replay them time and time again. This enables us to carefully watch, remember and then reenact the events of the night in our waking lives. This is a great way to solve problems, receive new skills and break old destructive habits. Other people have strengths where we may have weaknesses. By their visiting in our dreams we are able to receive from their areas of strength. This helps us to see how to fortify or shore up areas of weakness in our lives.

The people that appear in our dreams represent themselves, gifts, qualities, strengths or weaknesses, but sometimes they represent characteristics in us that we are not using. These great qualities remain buried or hidden in us until we see them demonstrated in someone else who has the same outstanding characteristics. Subconsciously, we see ourselves mirrored in their image.

Sometimes our subconscious selects people to appear in our dreams that we have never met. We may have only seen them on the movie screen or in passing on the street. The villains or criminals that are pictured on the most wanted at the post office may break into our dreams because someone we know is acting just like their descriptions. Images of people can come from characters in the novels we read, myths, fables or fairytales or even newspaper stories. The brave heroes who have walked through the pages of history come to our rescue. Or a valiant white knight in shining armor sweeps us off our feet. He carries us to a protected shelter, delivering us from a fire breathing dragon. We find safety and comfort in his strong capable arms.

When we are feeling confused, needy, and depressed or down and out, a person we consider wise or spiritual may appear to bring us joy, comfort, wisdom or a needed solution to press on and endure a difficult season. Their dream presence brings hope of a good or prosperous future.

People we haven't seen for years may visit us unexpectedly, giving us the same sweet assurance they did when we were in our formative years. They may appear as a wise sage, a teacher, a counselor or a mentor who always gave us the support we needed at life's critical crossroads. Sometimes all we need is someone to listen to our ideas or problems, who believe in us. One who says, "I know you can do it! Just give it a try!" "I believe in you!" These encouraging words are all that is needed for us to begin to believe in ourselves again. Their words instill a new faith and a hope to step forward into new possibilities. Sometimes these friends from our long lost past remind us of inner gifts and qualities. They remind us we used to be more adventuresome and take chances back then. But we may be too retiring or reserved now. We have placed some of our gifts on a shelf. If we dust those gifts off and put them back to use in our waking lives, they will ignite a new excitement, fulfillment and joy. We only have one life to live, so let's make the most of every opportunity.

The people who visit us in our dreams are there for a reason. They have been chosen to bring a message, impart a gift, pass on some needed wisdom, reveal a hidden fear or give us needed support. Ask yourself why has this particular person been chosen to be in my dream? What is the spiritual implication or significance of their name? What are they wearing? What colors appear? What do they represent to me? What type of feeling, emotion or response do they trigger in me? If they stir positive emotions and feelings in us, they are messengers of hope and prosperity. Their presence in our dreams will bring increase and blessings. They are there to remind us to use our positive gifts, characteristics and attributes in life.

Learning to investigate the meanings of people's names when they show up in dreams is a very important concept to master. Determine the spiritual connotation and the inherent meaning of their name. Sometimes the meaning of their name or even a life scripture that is associated with the meaning of their name offers the key to unlock the dream's message.

How does the meaning of their name apply in your life? For example the name Jonathan means gift of the Lord or God's precious gift. *Psalms 92:4, "For you, Lord, have made me glad through Your work; I will triumph in the works of Your hands."*

The name David means beloved or lover of all. King David's life was one of a God seeker, a violent flow of divine desire. *1 John 4:16, "And we have known and believed the love that God has for us. God is love and he who abides in love abides in God and God in him.*

The Bible describes Jonathan and David as soul mates, which had an undying love for each other as best friends. Jonathan loved David more than himself. He loved David so much he was willing to lay his life down for David. He was willing to serve David, as God's choice for king, although Jonathan was the rightful heir to Saul his father, the king's throne. Greater love has no man than this: but to lay his own life down so his friend can prosper. Perfect love cast out the painful emotion that is brought on my fearing we will be rejected, betrayed or made to suffer or hurt.

If a person named Jonathan or David appeared in your dream you can expect a very positive increase in love in your relationships. Prosperity or 'triumph' will increase in your work. God will enable you to be a vital gift to people in your life.

Also, consider the person's countenance. How do they appear in the dream? How are they dressed? What colors are they wearing? Are they bright and happy with the light of God radiating out of them? Then most likely they are bearers of God's presence, good news and a favorable report.

But, if their countenance is dark, gloomy, shadowy or evil in appearance, they usually represent painful memories, negative experiences, sickness, disease or inappropriate, harmful reactions in life. They are in your dream as a warning. They represent bad habits or indicate that you are slipping back into a harmful reactionary system. You may be reacting out of your hurt or fear instead of responding in an appropriate manner to situations in your life. If we don't learn from our past mistakes and responses and change, we are doomed to repeat the same mistakes again.

Negative dream characters can represent negative habits, reactions, cycles and patterns. When they appear it is time to take a personal inventory. Search your heart to determine if there is any evil way in you. Once you recognize the source of the negative energy, you can make the appropriate changes. Negative energy results in sin, which can be comprised of false or destructive patterns of thinking, believing a lie as truth, speculating or imagining the worst about people in a situation. All of these negative reactions produce fear, which has a paralyzing affect in your life. Tearing down wrong ways of thinking and reacting will enable you to overcome negative counterproductive energy or destructive sin in your life.

For a complete comprehensive list of thousands of People Dream Symbols please avail yourself to Dream Encounters Symbol Volume I & III at www.BarbieBreathitt.com

What in the World Are You Wearing?

Clothing and apparel represents the current person we would like to display in our present situation to those around us. If clothing is scant, lacking or inadequate to cover us, we are feeling ill-prepared for the challenges life is sending our way. What if our feet are bare? This usually means our walk or forward motion in life is being hindered or we are grossly unprepared to step out on our own. We may feel embarrassed or uncomfortable with the quality or style of clothing we are sporting.

When we have outgrown our clothing and they are too tight to allow us freedom of movement, this indicates we are feeling restrained, restricted or limited by circumstances.

When special occasions come in our dreams, we often search for our favorite power suit but are unable to locate it in the cluttered closet. If we find ourselves dressed as a clown, jester or gypsy we often feel silly, like others are laughing at us or unconnected as we wander through life. The clothes we wear indicate the protective mantles, gifts, talents or abilities that are coming to light in our life.

For a comprehensive list of Apparel and Clothing Dream Symbols please avail yourself to Dream Encounter Symbols Volume I at www.BarbieBreathitt.com

So You Are Pregnant Again!

Congratulations! Pregnant dreams are a common theme, even among men. Anyone of any age or gender can appear pregnant in their dream. But it usually does not mean they are actually carrying an unborn baby in their womb. That is good news for all the men who don't have a physical womb. And for all the older ladies who have already raised their children and don't want to start over, you can breathe a sigh of relief too.

Dreams of being pregnant, when you are not physically pregnant; means you are pregnant with weighty, new, creative ideas, strategies, thoughts, expressions or beliefs. Something new is starting in your life. If you will embrace and nurture this new beginning, it will flourish and grow to full term. However, if you ignore, abandon, abort or starve this new creation or invention it will not thrive, but will soon die.

The nine months of pregnancy indicates you are in the planning stages. This is the time to brainstorm, gather your resources and to count the cost. It is time to sit down and calculate the expenditure in time, money and people resources to see if you have enough to complete your project. Otherwise after the foundations are laid, and the team is not there to help and support, you will draw ridicule and disappointment will result.

We all need people to be successful! Pregnancy is a picture of a new person being created and developed. People will lift us up to the next level of success and prosperity if we can plan accurately and communicate the vision clearly. Once the plans and strategies are made and the support systems are in place it is time for the baby to be birthed.

What if You Really are Pregnant?

Congratulations! You are going to be a mother! That is one of the greatest honors any woman can have bestowed upon her. You are bringing another life into this world. Who will they be? The possibilities are endless. But, you have an opportunity to help form that little life into something wonderful and amazing.

During pregnancy your dreams are more vivid, mainly because of the hormonal and biological changes you are experiencing. Sometimes you will have dreams about your unborn child. Some women are able to determine the gender of their child before the sonogram. During the early stages of pregnancy, usually in the first trimester, the woman will have mixed emotional feelings of great excitement and anticipation from being pregnant, especially if it is her first pregnancy. But, due to her lack of experience, dreams of fear, of not being a good mother, lack of skill or even the possibility of losing the baby, try to horn their way into her subconscious.

Pregnancy dreams take many different forms. Some dream of bright water filled balloons with fish or a wide open field of flowers in bloom or beautiful fruit laden trees. Others view a house that is under construction with a cottage or room being added. Your mother comes for a visit toting a baby bag with diapers in hand. Still others dream of a mother eagle pushing the eaglets out of the nest, cute cuddly puppies, and fish being spawned or bouncy kittens.

While the mother to be dreams of her new baby coming into the world, the new father is having his own dreams. His proven virility changes his identity. The father to be wonders if he will be a good father in addition to his responsibilities as a loving husband and a bountiful provider.

Men report dreams of temporarily being ignored, locked away and sometimes totally forgotten or even lost. They sense a shift in their relationship as the wife's attention, energies and focus consistently revolves around preparing for the arrival of the newest member of the family. The theme of being abandoned or deserted can continue long after the baby is born, especially if the husband thinks caring for the baby is women's work. If he doesn't take on an active role in the preparation process, by painting the nursery, hanging curtain rods and assembling the crib, he will feel lost or unneeded. It is important that the new father learns to care for the baby's needs, changing diapers, bottle feeding and rocking him to sleep; if he doesn't, he will continue to feel left out. Most men dream that the baby is a son to carry on their name. They want to bond with their son at sporting events or hunting wild game, especially after feeling abandoned by their wife.

For a comprehensive book of Sports and Recreation Dream Symbols please avail yourself to at www.BarbieBreathitt.com

DREAM INTERPRETER

Chapter 11
Puns and Word Plays

Have you ever met a punster? You know the guy who is the life of the party because he can make a play on any word or spin a phrase in different directions to get an expression of amusement. No matter what you say he is able to craft a pun or a joke as an expert wordsmith or artisan. He is good at thinking abstractly and pulling in humor from original statements or ideas to make everyone laugh. He entertains by adding his own imagination and creativity.

The same thing can happen in your dreams. Your mind is very quick and clever. It will create symbols to take the place of words or other objects. Puns are the entertaining or amusing usage of words with connected meanings or relevance. Puns are a form of word play with two or more meanings; they are intended to be humorous or rhetorical in their effect. They often have the same or similar sounds but a totally different designation or characterization. For example, Buffalo is a city in New York; a large shaggy mane bison or a state of baffled bewilderment. Cleave means to both separate and to cling to. Explosion can represent sudden unexpected growth or total destruction. One may enjoy shopping at a mall but be devastated if they are mauled by a bear. A plane can fly high above obstacles or represent a level place or someone who is as common as a plain Jane. Let us eat lettuce in our salads to keep our great figures. God is the greatest punster of all! He has a wonderful sense of humor. Holy Spirit uses puns in His symbolic dream language.

Puns

I was so poor when I was growing up, I couldn't even afford to pay attention.

How do you make antifreeze? Steal her blanket.

He couldn't tell his mother that he ate some glue. His tight lips were sealed.

Those who sling mud or throw dirt are sure to lose ground.

The principle responsibility for a child's education is apparent.

A small girl swallowed some coins and was taken to a hospital. When her grandmother telephoned to ask how she was doing the nurse said, 'No change yet'.

Children think their teachers and parents are never-minded and all no–ing.

Unborn twins are womb-mates.

Sibling rivalry is relative.

The little old woman who lived in a shoe wasn't the sole owner – there were several strings attached.

If all of the women left America it would be a stagnation.

Last night, I dreamt that I had written Lord of the Rings. My husband said I'd been Tolkien in my sleep.

An immigrant with a meager grasp on the English language struggled to give an explanation to the doctor of why his wife could not have children. First he said, "She is unbearable." Getting a raised eyebrow from the doctor he tried again, "She is impregnable." Finally he blurted out, "She is inconceivable and not worth barren."

That's a remarkable chair. Yeah, I know, it rocks.

Memories of water in the basement came flooding back.

Word Plays

Seeing a porpoise in your dream could represent your life purpose.

Red the color; read the book, reeds grow in the water

Bull to force your way in, bully, talk trash

Buffalo to stall, cause to fear, deceive, confuse, bully

Cord cordially, in one accord, walking in discord

Tail of an animal, end, conclusion; tale to tell a story, relation

Lock the door, water lock, catch, fasten, deadbolt

Level with me, tell the truth, measure something to see if it is level

Explosion sudden increase, blast, angry outburst, detonation

Plane that flies in the air; plain to make obvious or clear, plane level surface

Chapter 12
Food and Nutrition Dream Symbols

Everybody dreams but everyone may not remember their dreams. In fact, everyone has several dreams during a normal night of sleep. On average, you can dream four to seven dreams within a one to two hours span of time every night. Dreams are a vital and necessary part of maintaining one's mental health. A lack of dream activity may indicate a personality or mental disorder, or a protein, vitamin or mineral deficiency. God has designed the human body to communicate its physical, emotional and spiritual needs through dreams.

The food we dream about shows us the type of energy we are taking into our situations. Fruits help to feed our spirit with love, joy, peace, gentleness, longsuffering, meekness, temperance and self-control. Fruit and grain represent fertility or our ability to multiply positive things in our lives. Food in dreams usually represent new creative ideas, belief systems and contemplation or "food for thought," mentally digesting ideas, feeding your spiritual hunger by repeatedly communing with the goodness of God. In dreams strawberries represent the goodness of God, a friendship with God; healing; a special delight, a pleasure or reward; and can refer to various locations where strawberries are known to grow in abundance like in Oklahoma, Louisiana and Plant City, Florida.

The words we speak should be as sweet as honey in case we are ever required to eat them ourselves. If the food in our dream is stale, old or rotting, then we can expect foul play or things to be stolen or ill treatment to follow in a toxic, rotten atmosphere.

The way food is prepared is important because it demonstrates the process in which you are formulating, creating thought patterns or what you are feasting upon. Remember the saying, "You are what you eat! Garbage in will mean garbage out!"

Food is Essential

Food is an essential component for all of us. Food can represent a myriad of different things depending on the context of the dream. The type of food that appears, how it is prepared, preserved or served is also important. Food can metaphorically indicate an increase or decrease in hunger for love, desires for friendship, romance, sexual fulfillment or the general pleasures in your life being gratified.

Jesus is the "bread of life." His body was and still is represented by a loaf of bread. We see this symbolic prototype throughout various symbolic representations in Scripture. We remember the broken body of Jesus in communion as the bread is broken, dispersed and eaten by believers. Jesus walked and shared His heart with His disciples on the Emmaus Road. Though they heard profound revelation as He explained the Scriptures, and their hearts passionately burned within, they did not recognize Jesus. He desired to carry them farther than they had ever been before, into a new realm of spiritual understanding. It was not until they observed Jesus, as He blessed, broke, and gave them the loaf of bread, that suddenly their spiritually blinded eyes were opened to see Him in a fresh way. They finally recognized Jesus, seeing Him in the higher, resurrected form He had taken. This is an important lesson for us to remember. Every time Jesus comes to us, He comes in a new form. Jesus is the Creator; so He is always making things new. As we commune with Him in sweet fellowship and we partake of His blood and body, we learn to correctly discern His body. Each one of us is uniquely created in the image of God as a diverse part of the body of Christ. We are each distinctive, having our own individual personality and ways that we express God's gifts. The living Christ in us is the hope we have, to enter into the same glorious power that resurrected Christ from the dead.

Imagine seeing one massive Jesus, the body of Christ, made up of trillions of individuals from every race, color, tribe and nations of people who have ever, or will ever live, all fit together, moving as one. We each hold a specific place and function in His body. Some are eyes, others are ears, mouth, hands, feet, heart, or lungs, but we all are indispensable and have a specific purpose, for the body to function correctly.

When bread appears in your dream it represents the basic needs of life, natural and spiritual food. Bread represents the fresh Word of God; the body of Jesus that gives us life and provision. Man does not live by bread alone, but by every creative word that proceeds from the mouth of God. If you are not daily tapping into the Word of God, you are not receiving the spiritual nutrition or wisdom that is vitally important in order for your life's journey to proceed. Bread enables you to see beyond the natural, to rise above the old, and enter into the new. Once the disciples recognized Jesus, He disappeared from their sight, only to appear later in another higher form of glory. Revelation is the bread of life; without it we perish.

Fruit

When food appears in your dreams, depending on the type and conditions of the food, it represents physical, emotional and spiritual nourishment that will supply the necessary energy for life. In dreams peaches represent peace, joy, companionship, and wellbeing, pleasing to the Lord, the joy of the Lord is our strength; generosity; bridal hope. Fruit represents the fruit of the Spirit, which are love (oranges), joy (peaches) and peace (figs and peaches), patience (pears), kindness, revealed love (tomatoes), goodness (olives), faithfulness (grapes), gentleness (bananas), and self-control (grapefruits).

Fruit can also represent sensuality or the sin of temptation, as in the (apple), the forbidden fruit. But, apples can also represent the sweet breath of the Holy Spirit bringing freedom, good health; a tranquil, a peaceful spirit, and words of appreciation while applesauce represents childish nonsense. Apples have many wonderful attributes. They are high in fiber so they promote a healthy digestive system. Apples also reduce the risk of strokes and heart attacks if they are eaten regularly.

Blueberries assist the brain in producing dopamine, a neurotransmitter that enhances the memory; the bodies' coordination and general feeling of wellbeing. Blueberries also prevent the growth of breast cancer cells.

Cherries are a great natural sleep agent. Cherries contain a high level of a sleep hormone called melatonin that also acts like an antioxidant to protect cell membranes from damage. Cherries also help to kill cancer cells that would form in the pancreas, breast tissue and liver.

Cranberries have an agent called pro-anthocyanins that works to keep harmful bacteria from building up on the lining of the urinary tract so they prevent urinary infections. If you suffer from bladder infections drink eight ounces of cranberry juice a day. Cranberries are a rich source of self-healing phenols and they help prevent the formation of LDL cholesterol in the arteries.

When various fruits appear in your dream they represent the fruit of creation which is the fruit of God's work Ps.104:13; the resurrection of Jesus 1Cor. 15:20, 23; the Holy Spirit Rom. 8:23; the righteous person bears good fruit Pro. 31:31,

Ps.1:3; repentance; harvest; light; fruit of the Spirit; love, joy, peace, patience, kindness, goodness, faithfulness, gentleness, and self-control Gal.5:22-23; the Tree of Life bearing twelve fruits for the healing of the nations, abundant life Gen.1:11–12 healing of the Fall, Rev.22:1–2, Ezek.47:12; richness Jer.40:10,12; abundance Deut.30:9, 28:11;Divine blessing; the Promised Land linked to obedience, Ex.3:8,Num.12:27, Deut.8:8; a good or bad action resulting in offspring; fruit of the lips, prayer, worship Prov.12:14; primal sin in the Garden; pain, shame, darkness, thorns, thistles, tares, wormwood; strangles life; suffering; ultimate death; green fruit represents disenchantment emerges from impatience and hasty actions.

Meat

Meat represents something of substance that will supply strength, strong revelatory teaching or a mature word. Raw meat represents animalistic needs or urges, raw impulses or carnal earthly nature. Meat can represent obstacles that will cause discouragement if not overcome or conquered. Rotten meat represents a distortion of the truth that will degrade your psyche. It may also portend some health problems with your muscular system or an infection somewhere in your body that will stop proper mobility. To eat cooked meat foretells of uncovering the central truth or heart of a matter that will align with your core values. When eating a steak, determine how it is cooked; well done, medium, well or rare. Steaks can represent a need to use our God given instincts to 'stake' a claim on a new opportunity. There may be 'high stakes' or a risk involved; but if the job is done well you will gain substantial potency, might and favor.

Vegetables

Vegetables represent healthy pursuits, the fulfillment of something or the crop of your labors coming forth. If you observe yourself eating veggies, then health, wholeness and prosperity will be your reward. Green vegetables represent a potential growth and a fresh new expansion in our thought life beginning. However, if the veggies are withering, dried up, or decaying, a season of sorrow, grief or sadness is on the horizon. It is time to heed your dream's warning; make the necessary changes to improve your dietary intake to ward off negative health issues. Artichokes are rich in antioxidants which protect the liver against toxic buildup by reducing the LDL (bad) levels of cholesterol. Broccoli is loaded with vitamin C so it both boosts the immune system and fights off cancer. Broccoli is rich in fiber so it enhances a healthy digestive system and also helps to normalize blood pressure levels.

Frozen Food

Frozen foods are processed, prepared and pre-packaged, so they lack a lot of nutritional value. These perishable foods are insulated and frozen to preserve a previous season of time. Frozen foods may indicate that your salary or your ability to obtain more credit, loans or investments will be frozen or fixed at its current level. This could indicate you are being frozen out, rejected, and placed on reserve, preserved for later use or possibly permanently suspended because of inflexibility. Frozen foods represent frigid ways of doing things or cold hearted emotions. Frost or freezer bite represents localized destruction; being stuck in a damaged, hurt, or ruined state of existence, incapable of acting or reacting. Eventually this icy, formal condition will kill your relationships. To see freeze-dried food means you are caught in a quick acting vacuum that will suck out every ounce of energy and leave you high and dry.

To dream of hoarding or amassing food represents a fear of spiritual, emotional or physical starvation or deprivation. Trust God to supply your daily needs. God will bear your burdens, give you grace and mercy, supply your daily portion of food, and forgive your sins as you forgive those who wrong you. If you ask Jesus, He will meet all your needs and keep you from evil.

If you see yourself eating old, stale food there is a need to reenergize and rejuvenate yourself. You need a change of routine, some fresh new ideas, input or challenges to make your life exciting. You have become bored with your existence. Your creativity is lacking or lethargic. You are emotionally or physically exhausted. Your spiritual life is dry, musty and outdated. You are living on yesterday's revelation. It is time to seek God for a fresh encounter, reflect on the Scripture daily. Shed the old appetites of times past and allow God to recreate a new hunger in you. Let the old pass away and behold the new things God has for your life. Embrace and ingest the necessary changes.

Depending on the type of dream food you are ingesting, notice the character traits or nutritional value of that particular food. Will introducing it into your diet improve your health and energy levels? To feast on ill-tasting food in a dream foretells of some bitterness, anger, or offense in your heart.

To see or eat burnt food in your dream indicates that you are experiencing some extreme rage, antagonism, resentment or stuffed emotions. An emotional overload is really 'smoking' or 'toasting' you. Your excessive emotions are draining your energy by zapping your vitality, strength or zest for life.

Baby Food

Babies are very dependent and need full-time care to receive their nutrients. They must be nurtured and hand fed. Baby food is soft and bland, easy to swallow because babies have not developed teeth or a strong digestive system. Teeth represent an ability to make decisions, gain wisdom or mull over a situation. To observe oneself eating baby food can indicate you are eating too much or gaining weight. Cut down on your intake by eating smaller or baby portions. You may also feel as if someone is hand feeding you small bits of information, slowly training you on some elementary principle you have already mastered; while treating you like an unlearned, infantile person.

Eating alone indicates independence; suggests a single lifestyle, a loss of a significant other, suffering from loneliness, or depression. There may be feelings of rejection, exclusion, or being cut off from friends, society or family ties.

Have you heard the expression "comfort food?" If your dream themes revolve around an excessive amount of eating; you may be replacing a loss of camaraderie with food consumption. Overeating and gluttony indicates self-absorption, greed, an excessive or ravenous appetite or a lack of discipline, self-respect or reaching out to others.

On the contrary starving yourself in dreams, by not eating enough or totally refusing food, may signify self-hatred, a lack of spiritual interest, or a need for divine participation. If you are dieting in real life your body may be screaming, "Feed me!" because your calorie intake has been decreased. Have you isolated yourself because some apprehension or anxiety is "eating at you?" Refusing to eat what others offer signifies you have a need for more independence and will reject attempts by others to control your life. You are a decisive person, who rarely asks for the opinions, suggestions or input of others. Picky eaters are very selective; they choose to embrace only the very best.

A dream of eating with people connotes synchronization, a bringing together of a harmonious life, close familiarity, festiveness, prosperity, personal, financial and spiritual expansion, and a merry heart.

To dream the dishes on the table are cleared away or your plate of food is removed, before you finish eating indicates those around you are trying to starve you out. Look for troubles and competitive issues to arise from a needy, calculating group of dependents.

Dreams of fast food points to the fact that you are not taking the time to properly care for your physical, emotional or spiritual health. You are looking for a shortcut or a quick fix that leads to sloppy results, while settling for scraps or whatever bag is being handed you. Sacrificing your future wellbeing on the altar of immediate gratification will mean a long term loss. Along the same lines, eating from food vending trucks in your dreams indicates that you are not catering to or allowing quality time to foster emotional welfare.

While some enjoy eating leftovers, others refuse to reheat the same food again. To dream of eating leftovers can mean you are still clinging to past resentments or the familiar. It's time to clear your plate in the garbage, and move on with a new, fresh, healthy start.

Although food fights are a lot of fun, they also indicate a clash or messy disagreement between two opinions or philosophies. The natural kingdom may be at war with the spirit realm, trying to force a violent resolve, or a physical response is in direct conflict with one's sentiments in waking life.

A food processor indicates a desire to find a more appropriate way to understand or "process" emotional responses by applying a more efficient technique or method.

To dream of eating plastic or toy food indicates you are not satisfied in your current level of communication. Facts are being inflated to cover up something. You are not being told the truth in an emotional relationship. Your significant other is not supportive; they are not being real or genuine. Their interactions are plastic or fake and do not meet your emotional needs.

To eat your pet's food in your dream alludes to a need to address and correct some rude, uncultured, ancient animal-like thought patterns before they become actions. If your pet is a dog, you may be battling thoughts of infidelity or questioning loyalty issues in the relationship. If the pet is a cat, you may be acting catty or in an overly independent manner.

Many edible sea creatures are bottom dwellers. They are considered unclean because they are used to filter and decontaminate the animals waste in the seawater. To see or eat seafood in your dream indicates the acknowledgment of your spiritual being, intergrading with your wakeful consciousness. There is a necessity to recognize your subconscious desires need to be fulfilled in a healthier manner. Seafood can also be a pun symbolizing "seeing food."

Milk

Have you ever felt like someone is "milking" you emotionally or financially? To see yourself milking a cow represents great opportunities are at hand; as long as you persevere and continue to work the situation, your bucket will overflow with blessings. Look for favor and opportunities to prosper. To see another milking a cow is a warning. Be aware of someone trying to take advantage of your generosity. They intend to milk you for all your worth. Have you every spilled you're milk in a dream? This foretells of a lost opportunity, a lack of trust or your faith failing. You will experience a loss or temporary setback or unhappiness arising from deceit.

Milk represents the elementary, simple, teachings of life that are foundational for early growth and spiritual nourishment. Although milk is wonderful to sustain a baby, it is an inferior diet for an adult as many have developed an allergic reaction to milk products. To observe a baby nursing, being lovingly nurtured on their mother's milk symbolizes the kindhearted care, integrity and compassion of the maternal instinct. Whole milk represents sensuous, pleasant, hospitable experiences.

To dream of drinking a glass of cold milk indicates harmony in the family and emotional nourishment. A cup of warm milk indicates you should ready yourself to receive hospitality and stop falling asleep on the job. Hot milk implies one's need to quietly strengthen outside relationships to increase their comfort level. To observe yourself giving milk away indicates you have a generous, benevolent heart. Large vats or containers of milk indicate wealth and abundant prosperity while dealing in commerce.

Buttermilk indicates new ideas of prosperity are churning in your head. Distress or trouble will follow a season of ease or pleasure. Churning milk signifies a difficult task will be set before you, but with much skill, and continued diligence, you will succeed.

Curdled, spoiled, sour, contaminated milk that leaves a bad taste in your mouth indicates the involvement of impure motives. You may have a sour outlook on life because friends have caused distress. You need to disengage from maintaining or supporting some relationship.

To take a refreshing milk bath means you can let down your guard and relax. You are in a beautiful season where you are safely encircled by faithful friends who will cover your back. Bathing in milk may indicate a need for mothering, but it also denotes an ability to create a kinship in pleasures, taking a beauty bath or cutting your teeth on the blessings of Judah's princes in a life of luxury. You are being given an opportunity to experience the fertile abundance of milk and honey flowing in the Promised Land.

To choke on milk indicates someone is babying you or being overly protective.

Their mothering nature is suffocating you. Chocolate milk indicates your life is very sweet at the moment. It is time to indulge in the new opportunities as they are presented.

Food Can Talk

Our bodies have been fearfully and wonderfully created. Our natural body is able to heal itself if it is given the proper food, supplements, minerals and quality nutrition. The body is also able to communicate its needs to us if we are attentive and play close attention to its subtle messages. We yawn when we are tired or sleepy. We cough when something tickles our throat. We gag when something is caught in our throat. We blink when a particle gets in or around your eye. When we dream, our bodies also communicate vital information to us. Everything that God creates communicates His great love to us. God paints colorful pictures in our dreams that reveal His ability to care for our every need through the things He has supplied for us in nature. Have you ever thought it was funny when a person said, "Your steak is so rare it is still mooing every time you cut into it?" Although that may just be a fun expression– food really can talk in your dream life.

God's Amazing Food Pharmacy

God's astute wisdom is revealed in His mathematical arrangement of fruit sections and segments, as well as in the number of grains. All grains are found in even numbers on the stalks, so every stalk of wheat has an even number of grains. The Lord specified in Matthew 13:23, that the seed that falls on good ground, people who hear His teaching and understand their parabolic meaning, will grow to produce a good crop thirtyfold, sixtyfold, and a hundredfold all even numbers. Each ear of corn has an even number of rows. A watermelon has an even number of stripes on the rind. Oranges have an even number of segments. A bunch of bananas has on its lowest row an even number of bananas, and each row decreases by one, so that one row has an even number and the next row an odd number.

God has designed specific foods with their mineral and vitamin components to heal designated tissues and organs in the body. Have you ever noticed that a cross-section of a carrot looks like the human eye, with a pupil inside the iris, including its radiating lines? Carrots enhance blood flow, which improves the visual function of the eyes. Carrots are packed with antioxidant compounds, and vitamin A, and carotenes. They help protect against cardiovascular disease and cancer. If carrots appear in your dream, your body is giving you a symbolic message, letting you know your physical or spiritual vision needs to be enhanced. Your eyes need to be opened to see a new dimension in a relationship or a business opportunity. Maybe you are blind to a situation that will cause harm if you do not open your eyes and see behind the scenes. It could also indicate some health issues concerning your vision, such as glaucoma, retinitis, macular degeneration or some other malady. To see a carrot in your dream indicates abundance and fertility, perseverance will bring plenty; prosperity; blessings; the pun to lure as in to 'dangle a carrot,' to bring motivation. To eat a carrot indicates clarity of vision is coming. You will see things more clearly.

The human heart has four crimson chambers. When we cut a tomato in half, we can see that it also has four red chambers. Tomatoes are full of lycopene which nourishes the heart and improves the quality of our blood. Lycopene is the essential ingredient that makes tomatoes, watermelon and grapefruit look red. It is a powerful anti-oxidant and has defensive effects against both cardiovascular disease and cancer.

To see tomatoes in your dream could indicate you are suffering from issues that are causing your heart some duress. It is time to ask God to heal your broken or ailing heart. It may also be time to schedule a stress test with your physician. Tomato dreams may indicate that your heart is not functioning at full capacity. You may be grieving, disappointed or feeling rejected as a failure. Please note there was a time when people hurled rotten tomatoes to show contempt for a poor performance.

On a more positive note, tomatoes grow on a vine where they are clearly seen by everyone so they represent revealed love, kindness or generosity. To see a vine ripe tomato indicates domestic happiness is growing to its full potential. The dreamer is enjoying the fruit of emotional, physical, spiritual and relational harmony. To eat tomatoes prophesies good health. The major tomato growing states are Tennessee, Arkansas, Florida and California; so one of these various states may be coming into focus in your life.

Grapes grow on vines; which remind me of the intricacies of our circulation system. When grapes are mature they hang in a cluster that has the same shape as a heart. Each grape is round like a blood cell. Grapes are nutritious because they revitalize the heart, blood and circulatory system. Grapes are rich sources of vitamins A, B6, C, in addition to essential minerals like potassium, calcium, iron, phosphorus, magnesium and selenium. Grapes are very powerful antioxidants. To see grapes in a dream indicates opulence, wealth, the spirit of promise is coming to pass because of faithfulness and the fullness of time; and that you have been abiding in the vine. When the dreamer is eating grapes he can expect an abundance, (Amos 9:13) decadence and great prosperity because hard work will bring forth a rich harvest. You will be successful. Grapes represent fortitude and the ability to present pleasure, the celebration of fertility bringing forth fruitfulness. To pick or gather grapes represents a significant profit and fulfillment of goals and desires. In Song of Solomon 7:12, grapes of the vineyard are used as a way to picture the lover's invitation to intimacy. People's obedience or disobedience is linked to a blessing or their punishment by judgment. The failure of grapes to mature means disaster, or the premature casting off by the vine leads to the demise of the wicked Job 15:33, because of their waywardness Isaiah 5:2–4. When a person sins, it brings forth evil, wickedness and injustice which is represented by "sour grapes" (Jer. 31:29–30) sin sets a person's teeth on edge. An angel wielding a sharp sickle harvest (Rev. 14:18–19) the clusters of grapes from earth's vine and throws them into God's great winepress of wrath. Grapes also represent one's immortality and the sacrifices one has to make in life.

A walnut looks like the left and right hemispheres of a brain's upper cerebrums and lower cerebellums. The wrinkles or folds of the walnut resemble the neocortex. When eaten on a regular basis, walnuts help develop more than three dozen neuron-transmitters for proper brain function. Walnuts are rich in fiber, B vitamins, magnesium, and antioxidants, such as Vitamin E, all which contribute to making the body healthy! In dreams, the walnut indicates intellectual thought spent towards a difficult undertaking. When the task is done one will find favor, abundance and experience great joy. If the walnut is cracked potential opportunities will fail. When different kinds of nuts appear in your dream it is time to know and understand the inside workings; to attain success, favor, love, and prosperity. Be aware of those who are acting crazy or out of their mind. What is the motivation behind their nutty behavior? It could be difficult to discern or understand; "This is a hard nut to crack".

Kidney Beans are shaped precisely like the human kidneys. Next time you visit the salad bar; add some kidneys beans, they actually heal and help maintain proper kidney function. Kidney beans are rich in micro-elements and co-enzymes, namely the molybdenum and iron. Their high dietary fiber helps reduce cholesterol and help stabilize high blood sugar. The kidney participates in regulating blood pressure, the acid-base balance of electrolytes, homeostasis, and the hormone and endocrine systems. Our kidneys function as detoxifiers and as the body's filter. If you dream of a kidney, your body or soul is in need of cleansing, or you may need to filter through some painful issues that are acting like stones clogging up your forward momentum or successful flow.

Beets are full of folic acid which helps prevent LDL cholesterol formation, and is a B vitamin which protects against heart disease and cancer. To see beets in a dream means a plentiful yield coming from a good root; foundation of peace; encouragement; word play on "beats me."

Celery, bok Choy, rhubarb and many more stalk type vegetables look like the bones of our skeletal system. Bones are 23% sodium, so these foods contain 23% sodium so they replenish, increase or maintain bone strength. If you don't have enough sodium in your diet, the body removes it from the bones, thus your bones lose density and become weak or brittle.

Celery provides an excellent source of vitamin C and fiber. It is a very good source of folic acid, potassium, & vitamins B1. Dreams of celery indicate the dreamer is flourishing and has found prominence, wealth and riches, health, love and affection. To see celery appear in your dream indicates you may need to purify you body and cleanse your emotions. It could also be a pun on the word, "salary" representing some financial concerns or difficulties.

To see rhubarb growing in your dream means increased pleasures and prosperity. To cook rhubarb in a dream means you have a strong opinion that will lead to a heated argument. If you are eating it, your situation is not gratifying. Your frustration will lead to a job change. Chicory is a close cousin to the endive and escarole. A quarter cup of raw chicory greens provides more vitamin A than any other salad green. Vitamin A comes from beta-carotene which is a potent self-healer that fights cancer, vital for a healthy immune system and protects your vision.

A combination of avocadoes, eggplant and pears improve the physical condition and function of the womb and cervix. Interestingly, their shapes resemble these female organs. If a woman eats one avocado a week, it will balance her hormones, help her shed unwanted birth weight, and help prevent cervical cancers. Note that it takes exactly nine months to grow an avocado from blossom to ripened fruit and it takes nine months for a baby to develop from conception to delivery. Avocados reduce cholesterol levels in the body. Avocados possess powerful antioxidants which help the body fight off cancer causing substances. If you dream of an avocado, you will be well pleased if you dedicate some more time and exert a greater amount of energy towards some ambition, aspiration or project.

When a pear appears in your dream it represents patience needed to possess the promise, health and hope; notice the color, it will indicate the measure your patience have developed or the level of your maturity.

To see oil in dreams indicates an anointing; God's blessing and favor; the Holy Spirit, a setting apart as a prophet, priest, or king; fertility; prosperity Deut. 32:13; oil is a staple or the essence of life, fuel that will propel the body and vehicles Matthew 25:3–8; a needed food; cosmetic enhancement; a medicine used for healing Ps. 23:5; James 5:14; indulgence; a great honor when you are anointed by others.

Coconut Oil is high in calories so one or two teaspoons a day gives you all the lauric acid you need to fight viruses and bacteria in the body.

Olives look like ovaries and they improve the ovaries health and ability to ovulate. Olives are helpful to diabetic patients because it can control your blood sugar because it is high in monounsaturated fat. It can also help to prevent colon cancer, and gastritis. Olives represent the oil of anointing that causes the presence of light, the favor and the "or" of God to rest on an individual. To see or eat olives means healing medicine, health and gratification, immortality, true to life friends, and a prosperous business. To see an olive branch or tree indicates righteousness, Israel and the Tree of Life. There will be reconciliation by the bringing together of peace, hope and resolution of conflicts in relationships. To wear or see a crown of olive leaves represents that an old burden will be lifted; you will triumph over impediments, and victoriously end a conflict.

Citrus fruits such as oranges, tangerines, limes and lemons and grapefruit as well as their juices, support the health of mammary tissue by increasing the flow of lymph removing the toxins from the breast. Look at a cross-section of an orange it looks like the inner makings of a woman's breast tissue. Citrus fruit contain many essential vitamins, C, D and B6, B5 (pantothenic acid), and minerals, including: calcium, phosphorous, potassium, and niacin. They prevent heart disease and promote the health of bones, ligament, muscle and skin. Citrus also improves your mood and cognitive functions.

In a dream a lime represents fleeting distresses; adversity will cause increased success; but limes also represent refreshing; enhancement so put your limes in a coconut and drink it all up and you will feel better in the morning.

When oranges appear in a dream they speak of love, the kiss of the Son, Ps. 2:12, "son kissed oranges." To see or eat an orange represents the inspiration of the senses in life, springing up in a new hope. One is being friendly, courteous, or a generous giver in many areas. You are very sociable with an extroverted nature; it's time to broaden your goals. Exploring new horizons will increase your significance.

Grapefruit foretell of self-control. To eat a grapefruit indicates a state of health, rejuvenation, security, welfare and happiness. You are in high spirits; a good emotional state of mind. A grapefruit tree represents your many talents, gifts, abilities, as well as your positive thought structure. Since it is a fruit it also represents the harvest from your good deeds and hard labor. What you have invested in others will return to bless you

Jesus cursed the fig tree when it didn't produce any fruit. The fig tree was full of leaves to hide behind, but it was sterile or barren of fruit, unable to reproduce. In

Genesis 1:28–31, the Bible records that, *"God blessed them (Adam and Eve); and God said to them, "Be fruitful and multiply, and fill the earth, and subdue it; and rule over the fish of the sea and over the birds of the sky and over every living thing that moves on the earth." Then God said, "Behold, I have given you every plant yielding seed that is on the surface of all the earth, and every tree which has fruit yielding seed; it shall be food for you; and to every beast of the earth and to every bird of the sky and to every thing that moves on the earth which has life, I have given every green plant for food; and it was so."*

As figs grow they are full of seeds and hang in twos like the male testicles. Figs increase the number and mobility of male sperm so they help men to overcome sterility. Figs are beneficial when used in the treatment of sexual debility. They can be supplemented by other dry fruit, like dates along with almonds and butter. Figs are an excellent source of potassium, dietary fiber and manganese. Manganese helps to control infertility, sexual weakness, heart disorders, memory loss, and muscle contractions. Figs are considered a restorative food which helps in quick recovery after prolonged illness. Figs restore the body after physical and mental exertion. Figs endow the body with renewed vigor and strength. In dreams figs represent peace, prosperity, solitude, and communion with God. Figs are a delicacy so they foretell of recovering plunder; a positive, affirmative turn bringing more provision and a favorable return to health, 2 Kings 20:7; profit and wealth. To see good figs, (Jer.24:5–7) means that God's eyes are watching over people to bring them back to a place of knowing Him. If they will return to God He will build them up and not tear them down. God will sow and plant them so that they will not be uprooted.

To see bad figs (Jer.24:9–10) means there is an abhorrent, offense to all. They are in danger of becoming a reproach, a byword, an object of ridicule, receiving a curse due to deception. There is a risk of being banished; falling under the sword of judgment, famine or plague will destroy their self-efforts. To see a fig leaf indicates one's effort to cover up their shame and nakedness; due to a loss of innocence. They need to repent of an apathetic attitude ("I don't give a fig!"; "Not worth a fig!") and receive God's grace.

To dream of dates represents prosperity; happiness; joy and fun; courtship; time is significant, pay close attention to past, present and future "dates", notice the duration of something; an engagement to go out socially or to enjoy a performance is coming soon.

In dreams almonds represent health; gifts; authority; happiness; offering your best; Gen.43:11; diligence and hard work will result in increased production, harvest and profits resulting in wealth, God's choice; success and financial gain;

Num.17:8; God's faithfulness, awakening Jer.1:11–12.

Sweet potatoes are shaped like the pancreas. Diabetics can eat sweet potatoes without worry as these tubers have a low glycemic index. Sweet potatoes contain vitamin A, vitamin C, manganese, magnesium (anti-stress, relaxation mineral), high fiber, B6 vitamins which prevent heart attacks; potassium and even iron. Antioxidants have anti-inflammatory properties which makes sweet potatoes an excellent food for those suffering from either arthritis or asthma. Vitamin D supports the thyroid; and plays a vital role in our energy levels, moods, and helps to build healthy bones, heart, nerves, skin, and teeth. Sweet potatoes also contain the mineral iron, which helps us sustain sufficient vigor, produce red and white blood cells, resistant anxiety, boost proper im¬mune functions, and metabolize protein. In dreams sweet potatoes represent humility, unity, and a staple that brings balance and harmony. To see or eat a sweet potato in your dream suggests that you have a strong libido. You may need to find a compromise in order to make the marriage relationship mutually comfortable and satisfying for both parties if your mate's libido does not match yours. Mashed potatoes are a favorite at meal time. In dreams potatoes represent concealed love because they grow under the ground where they are not seen by anyone but God's watchful eye. When potatoes are cooked, beaten and mixed together in one pot it is impossible to discern which potato was part of another they all blend together for one corporate purpose to nourish the body.

Onions look like the body's cells. Research has determined that onions help remove waste materials from all of the body cells. They also increase tear production to cleanse the epithelial layer of the eyes. The onion is the richest dietary source of quercitin. Quercitin is a sedative, potent antioxidant flavonoid that is found on and near the onion's skin. Quercitin is an anti-inflammatory, antibiotic, antiviral, which is thought to have diverse anti-cancer powers because it specifically inhibits human stomach cancer. It also thins the blood, lowers cholesterol, raises good-type HDL cholesterol, and wards off blood clots. If you have coronary disease, you should eat onions daily. Onions also fight asthma, chronic bronchitis, hay fever, diabetes, atherosclerosis and infections. The amino acids and vitamin C found in onions detoxify the body from heavy metals, lead and arsenics. Garlic is a great workmate of onions that helps eliminate toxins and the free radicals that endanger the body. To dream of onions causing tears means you will have to persevere through others' jealousy, disagreement, and hurtful words. Be genuine, don't be fake or phony, and stop using deceit. Dig deeper for manifold levels of revelation and answers to problems, they will resolve conflict and bring needed spiritual insight. Revelation and understanding comes level by level. There are multi-layered issues coming into new knowledge and insight that will unveil self-discovery to benefit the world (Egypt). If you observe an onion halved and strategically displayed around the house in your dream, this could indicate the air in your home or work environment has become polluted with toxins. Onions are one of nature's greatest filters and can catch and absorb germs.

For an extensive comprehensive list of Nutrition dream symbols and their meanings, please avail yourself of *Barbie's Dream Encounter Symbols Volume 2* at htpp://www.BarbieBreathitt.com

Pharaoh's Grain and Cattle Dreams

Pharaoh saw himself standing by the Nile River in his dream. He saw seven fat sleek cows that were swallowed up by seven ugly and gaunt cows, and then he awoke. He fell back to sleep and dreamed a second dream. *"Now it happened at the end of two full years that Pharaoh had a dream, and behold, he was standing by the Nile. And lo, from the Nile there came up seven cows, sleek and fat; and they grazed in the marsh grass. Then behold, seven other cows came up after them from the Nile, ugly and gaunt, and they stood by the other cows on the bank of the Nile. The ugly and gaunt cows ate up the seven sleek and fat cows. Then Pharaoh awoke."*

The Scriptural principle of doubles comes into play here. God will often speak twice, send two dreams or call a person's name twice to get their attention. The Bible gives us several examples of God calling His servants' names twice. When God spoke a name twice it indicated a calling or setting apart of that person, a warning, a change or transition into a new era being established. Abraham, the friend of God, was prevented from sacrificing Isaac, *Genesis 22:11*, Samuel's eyes and ears were awakened to the voice of God *1 Samuel 3:10*, Simon Peter was warned of the devil's plot to sift him in *Luke 22:31* and Saul is changed into Paul *Acts 9:4* who developed into a man who's soul desire was a burning passion to know Christ.

Here we see that the Pharaoh's dream repeated the message of the first dream but used grain, a different symbolism to help communicate the same message clearly.

Grains refer to a cycle of planting seed, giving it time to grow so it reaches maturity before the harvest. One seed will bring forth an abundance of new seeds. When the seed is planted it will bring forth a large and prosperous harvest of ideas, relationships or whatever we have sown our time into. Seeds bear seeds after their own kind. *"Then God said, "Let the earth sprout vegetation, plants yielding seed, and fruit trees on the earth bearing fruit after their kind with seed in them"; and it was so. The earth brought forth vegetation, plants yielding seed after their kind, and trees bearing fruit with seed in them, after their kind; and God saw that it was good." Genesis 1:11–12 NASU*

"While the earth remains, seedtime and harvest, and cold and heat, and summer and winter, and day and night shall not cease." Genesis 8:22 NASU

When a dream repeats itself using similar language it means that the dream is being established and will soon take place. *Genesis 41:25, 32* God will establish something with a witness of two. God sent His disciple out in teams of two because there is safety and great power in two coming into spiritual agreement. This is also why the enemy comes against marriages to destroy their power of agreement *Matthew 18: 18–20, Ecclesiastes 4:9–12*.

In the second dream, God chose to speak to Pharaoh about famine through the symbolism of both plump and scorched grain. God clearly communicated the duration of the famine again by using the symbolism of seedtime and harvest. *"He fell asleep and dreamed a second time; and behold, seven ears of grain came up on a single stalk, plump and good. Then behold, seven ears, thin and scorched by the east wind, sprouted up after them. The thin ears swallowed up the seven plump and full ears. Then Pharaoh awoke, and behold, it was a dream. Now in the morning his spirit was troubled, so he sent and called for all the magicians of Egypt, and all its wise men. And Pharaoh told them his dreams, but there was no one who could interpret them to Pharaoh." Genesis 41:1–8*

The commerce of Egypt revolved around the Nile River. Crops were planted on a yearly cycle, thus the seven stalks represented seven years. Crops were watered and harvested depending upon the rise and fall of the Nile's flood plains.

Cattle need both water and grain to be healthy. Cattle are bred, birthed and mature at a certain time of the year. Yearlings are sent to market and the owner reaps a great gain of prosperity. Thus the two sets of seven cows also represented a seven year cycle of plenty; followed by an additional seven year cycle of famine.

Nothing on earth can survive without water and plant life. When the heavens are shut there is no rain, which brings drought and famine. Famine affects drastic changes to the kingdoms of man, plant, animal and the economic world systems. Famine always brings lack and death. God was warning Pharaoh to prepare during the seven years of plenty for a great famine that was coming upon the world.

Just as God used dreams in the times of the ancient Pharaohs to foretell that which He had planned to bring upon the earth; the dreams we have today, also let us know, what will happen in our lives. God does nothing upon the earth without first telling His servants the prophets through dreams and visions.

Learning to understand the language of dreams will help you prosper and understand the things that remain hidden from those who do not seek to know God in this intimate manner of communication. Visions are one of the ways God has chosen to make Himself known to us. Learning to interpret dreams is vital to our continued success and ability to prosper in the dark and the glorious days that are coming upon the earth. Seek God's face with all your heart and He will be found of you.

Author Bio

Dr. Barbie L. Breathitt is a certified Prophetic Dream Life Coach, an author, ordained minister, dedicated educator, a gifted spiritual Seer, and respected teacher of the Divine supernatural manifestations of God. Barbie's dynamic teaching skills, intelligence, and quick wit make her a favorite with audiences everywhere. Through prayer, intense study, and years of research, Barbie has become the recognized leader in dream interpretation and has equipped people in more than 40 nations around the globe. Her prophetic gifting and deep spiritual insights have helped multiplied thousands of people understand the diverse ways God speaks to us today. Barbie has degrees from Southeastern University and Abraham Baldwin Agricultural College. Barbie earned her Ph.D. from Tabernacle Bible College and Seminary. Through her tangible faith and motivating life stories, Barbie challenges her audience to dive into the deeper mysteries of God with the anticipation of hearing His voice clearly and experiencing the touch of His presence. Her desire is to span denominational boundaries and bridge the gap between the secular realm of truth seekers with a clear message of hope, signs, and wonders, and the demonstration of the power of God. Her passion in life is to help individuals pursue their understanding of a loving God and to find their highest purpose and destiny in Him.

MYONAR.COM

Barbie Breathitt Enterprises is excited that so many people in God's Kingdom are exploring the understanding of dreams. We've opened an interactive Web site called MyOnar.com, "MyDream" which is impacting dreamers all over the world. Onar means "dream" in the Greek language and the book of Matthew records five unique onars (dreams). We believe it is vitally important to record God-given dreams and to search out the messages they contain. Sign up for your free online dream journal at www.MyOnar.com. From the dream journal, you can easily submit your dreams for interpretation by Barbie and our superlative dream interpreters.

Dream Encounters–Seeing Your Destiny from God's Perspective is the "Rosetta Stone" to interpreting the illusive vapors of dreams. Uniquely inspired, and written to convince the greatest skeptics, and educate the most ardent believer, "Dream Encounters" will bring God's perspective, and understanding to the symbolic, visual, love letters, in the mysterious world of dreams. Take a journey into the sub–conscious night parables of the soul, to learn how dream truths impact your world; give direction, purpose, and destiny. Gain valuable keys to success by unlocking the mysteries of your dreams. Available as a paperback book, digital book or audio book.

Dream Encounter Anointing Oil Anoint yourself every night with this fragrant dream enhancing oil and pray for the Holy Spirit to visit you in your sleep. You will experience a heightened level of dreams, visions and visitations from the Spirit of God.

The Encounter Series, a wonderful series of messages on CD's, mp3's and DVD's, is about learning, impartation, activation and encountering the realm of the Spirit where you will learn to do the work of the ministry. Our encounter training manuals and spiritual activities are designed to help you build confidence to go out and do the works of the kingdom, fulfilling your destiny and call.

DREAM INTERPRETER

**The Dream Encounter CD and Manual** is designed to teach, train, activate, and impart the skills to interpret and understand how God communicates to us through dreams and visions of the night. Jesus continues to teach through night parables, in other words, inspired dreams. The Bible gives us three keys that will be used in the end-time revival and outpouring of the Holy Spirit. The course topics include: Dreams, Visions, Transportations, Translations, Lucid Dreams, Colors, Numbers, Dream Symbols, Dream Interpretation, and Dream Teams and Outreaches.

**The Dream Encounter Workshop 5 DVD Series** Watch Barbie as she shares about God's dream language. She shows you valuable techniques to diagram your dreams, and how to follow the Holy Spirit's lead as he unlocks the secrets that reveal their hidden meanings.

**Colorado Dream Encounter Workshop 10 DVD Series** Topics include: Realm of the Spirit, Dream Resources and Tools, Introduction to Dreams, Biblical Foundations of Dreams, Dream Diagramming Techniques, Hindrances to Dreams, Recurring Dreams, Night Mares, Dreams & Visions, Sources and Types of Dreams, Recording and Interpreting Dreams, Impartation Prayer, Four Phases of Sleep, Purposes of Spiritual Dreams, God's Colors of Light, Power of Words, Creating Symbol Dreams, Visual Illusions, God's Symbols, Can You Read This?, and God's Numbers in Dreams.

**The Revelatory Encounter CD and Manual** is a prophetic course designed to teach, train, activate, and impart the ability to hear God's voice for yourself and others. This training helps you recognize and remove hindrances to hearing God's still, small voice. The course topics include: Developing Godly Character and Integrity, Old and New Testament Prophets, False Prophets, Immature Prophets, God's Friends, Knowing God's Voice, Difference between the Gift of Prophecy and the Prophetic Office, Forms of Revelation, Four Categories of Prophecy, Spirit of Prophecy, Nine Gifts of the Holy Spirit, Interpretation, Application, The Seer, The Watchmen, Intercession, Prayer, Intimacy, Spiritual Authority, and Developing Prophetic Ministry Teams.

**The Angelic Encounter CD and Manual** is a course that establishes a biblical foundation for the proof and ministry of angels. Topics include: What are Angels? Ministry of Angels; Types, Functions, and Characteristics of Angels; Satan and Fallen Angels; and Angels and the Death of the Saints. Barbie shares personal experiences of angelic visitations from her life.

**The Kingdom Encounter 12 CD Series** includes some of Barbie's most popular teaching topics The Cycle of Life, Inheriting the Kingdom of God I and II, The Power of Peace, Entering into Rest, It's Time for a Suddenly in Your Life, It's Raining, Pure Heart, Pure Light, Ezekiel's River and Wheels, Dressed for Success, Clothed in God's Light, The Kingdom Power of Change, God's Colors and Light.

**Dream Symbol Cards** These artistically designed dream symbol cards enable the dreamer to tap into the hidden meanings of the symbols that appear in many dreams and visions. These cards are also useful in helping the believer decipher the symbolic language that God uses to communicate through the revelatory realm of the Spirit. "God is speaking powerfully through dreams in this hour. So many believers are having significant dreams but do not always understand the significance of the symbols within them. Barbie Breathitt has done a marvelous job of preparing dream cards as a tremendous tool to help this process. They are very high quality and fully laminated for long-term use. I was impressed when I saw them." Patricia King XP Ministries www.xpministries.com

Acquire all of Barbie's artistically designed, laminated Dream Encounter Symbols Cards. They are available as single dream cards, in an excel spreadsheet or in spiral-bound collections.

- Volume I has the original 23 dream symbol cards.
- Volume II has 18 different dream symbol cards.
- Volume III has an additional 29 spiral bound dream symbol cards.
- Volume IV "ACTIONS" has 13 artistically designed spiral bound dream symbol cards.
- Dream Sexology has 4 unique and informative dream symbol cards that explain the meanings of your intimate symbolic dream language.
- When Will My Dreams Comes True? Dream Interpretation Nuggets, Times and Seasons
- Sports and Recreation contains 13 descriptive dream symbol cards

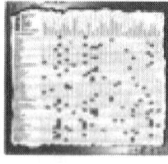**Healing Card** is a reference card that matches illnesses and diseases with possible spiritual root causes. This Healing card is birthed from Barbie's ministry experiences and encounters of seasoned intercessors and those in healing ministries. Great for intercessors and individuals who need clear direction for their healing prayers.

**Waking Words of Ancient Wisdom** Make it a practice to notice the time on the digital clock as you awaken from a spiritually significant dream. The numbers displayed on the digital clock are often keys to help understand the message God is giving you in your dreams. Note the time on your clock, then look up the corresponding chapter and verse in the Bible. Allow the Holy Spirit to quicken the intended "Waking Words of Ancient Wisdom" to your heart and apply them in your life. This is a wonderful way to daily explore the Bible while you seek the deeper meanings of the treasures God is revealing to you through your dreams. Visit www.BarbieBreathitt.com to obtain detailed directions for use.

*So You Want to Change the World?* is a compilation of twelve authors' perspectives on how you can make a positive difference in your world. Some key themes include: Doing the same things and expecting change. Church-as-usual isn't working. God can do amazing things with humble, broken vessels. The Secret Place is the key to hearing Heaven's heartbeat and bringing God's will to earth. Change can come through miracles, worship, and intercession. The essays reflect a variety of inspiring and exciting thought. You are encouraged and will be motivated to think and act beyond your normal routine and traditions--stretching yourself for the sake of bettering your world for His glory.

*Hearing and Understanding the Voice of God* Nine gifted and God-loving authors share their personal experiences on topics ranging from supernatural and out-of-body experiences in the third heaven to prophecy and discernment. You will quickly realize through reading these thrilling stories that hearing God happens in many different ways, and you can learn how you can tune in to Him yourself. Incredible things happen when you listen for God's voice—and when you ignore His promptings. Powerful and compelling stories challenge you into a deeper understanding about how to truly communicate with God.

*Gateway to the Seer Realm: Look Again to See Beyond the Natural* is written by Dr. Barbie Breathitt a gifted Seer who has years of personal experience interpreting dreams and ministering in the prophetic realm. You will gain valuable insights into understanding the ways of God and the divine supernatural realms of vision, dreams, angels, healing and destiny. Open new dimensions of revelation knowledge to learn how to access the Seer realm through intimate daily communication with God.

 ***Dream Seer: Searching for the Face of the Invisible*** is written by Dr. Barbie L. Breathitt to help the reader understand the Seer Realms of angels, divine visions, the voice and presence of the Lord and dimensions where the ethereal vapors of our dreams will become substantial presences when we believe that anything is possible with God. God is the giver of dreams. Jesus is also the Redeemer. So, like a knight in shining armor, He comes to restore the dreams we have allowed to fall by the wayside. The Holy Spirit inspires us to recall the images He sent long ago. God has mapped out our future. He brings the events of the world to bear on our individual circumstances as He wills. When the events of our lives coincide with the correct timing of His plans, the next phase of our destiny ensues. The Holy Spirit knows the perfect time to bring the dreams and plans He has formulated to enable our purpose to come to pass.

For these products and additional resources by Dr. Barbie L. Breathitt please visit
www.MyOnar.com
www.BarbieBreathitt.com
www.BreathoftheSpiritMinistries.com
www.BarbieBreathittEnterprises.com

Breath of the Spirit Ministries, Inc.
PO Box 820653
North Richland Hills, TX 76182-0653
(972) 253-6653

Copyright Material ©2014 Breath of the Spirit Ministries, Inc.
All reproduction specifically prohibited except by express written consent from Breath of the Spirit Ministries, Inc.
Barbie Breathitt
Breath of the Spirit Ministries, Inc.